Special Educational Needs and Disability (SEND) in practice

by Claudia Holmes and Claire Hewson

Contents

Published by Practical Pre-School Books, A Division of MA Education Ltd, St Jude's Church, Dulwich Road, Herne Hill, London, SE24 0PB.

Tel: 020 7738 5454 www.practicalpreschoolbooks.com

Associate Publisher: Angela Morano Shaw

Design: Mary Holmes **fonthill**creative 01722 717036

© MA Education Ltd 2020. All images © MA Education Ltd. All rights reserved.

Introduction

Children's right to thrive

A disability should not get in the way of a child enjoying a fulfilling life. All children should be able to take part in activities, feel included in educational settings and receive special care if needed. Children with special educational needs and disabilities (SEND) are not defined by their disability. Like all children they have the right to be treated as individuals and to make choices about their own life. They are entitled to receive every opportunity and encouragement to achieve their full potential.

Every child has the chance to thrive when they are valued and respected by others, and have the space to play and develop within a secure and caring environment.

To know that they are included, that others have high expectations of them, and that their achievements are celebrated helps them to build confidence and brings a sense of fulfilment.

It is crucial that positive attitudes towards all children should be embedded in the culture of every early years setting.

Children's experiences in the early years lay a solid foundation for their overall development and foster a thirst for learning. The early years shape the way in which children learn, get along with others and respond to life's challenges.

The important role of the early years practitioner

Children with special educational needs are everybody's responsibility, not just the SENCO's and the setting manager's. The SENCO's job is to support the practitioner to carry out their role for the benefit of the child.

Under the new Ofsted framework, SEND is no longer a separate category. This reflects the legal duty early years providers have to make sure that every child is fully included in all aspects of early years' provision.

Government guidance recognises that early years practitioners who interact with children day-to-day are often the first people to notice that a child has an emerging difficulty and they are the ones who implement provision to help them. By drawing upon their own observations, working with professionals within and sometimes outside the setting, talking to parents, and listening to the child themselves they will be able to implement timely, individually-tailored support. It is important to remember that the provision children receive now has long-term effects on every aspect of their development.

The purpose of this book is to help practitioners to secure the best possible outcomes for children with SEND and to make a positive, lifelong impact on families' lives. The aim is to give practitioners an in-depth, all-round knowledge of special educational provision in the early years. Chapter 2 gives a breakdown of the legislation that forms the basis of all SEND practice in this country and underpins the government's statutory guidance, 'Special educational needs and disability code of practice: 0-25 years' (the SEND Code).

The book is a practical, easy-to-use guide that can be read from cover to cover or dipped in and out of when needed. It guides practitioners through the special educational needs system and will help them with strategies to address children's specific needs. It will also signpost practitioners towards sources of information.

The SEND Code is very clear that early years practitioners must support parents to contribute to their child's education by listening to their views, making decisions with them, and by helping them to contribute towards special educational needs assessments. We hope that this book will place practitioners in a stronger position to fulfil this duty, but more than that, to be driven to go the extra mile for the benefit of children and their families.

Author Claudia Holmes' daughter, Sophie, has Down Syndrome and attends a mainstream infant school. Here, Claudia shares her experiences about the valuable role that practitioners play in the life of children with SEND and their families.

Claudia's story

Being a parent is the most exciting and complex role that any human being can experience, and being a parent of a child with special educational needs and disabilities isn't an exception. We are all warriors who will fight to the ends of the Earth for our child.

The difference is that when you are a parent with a child who has SEND, life can be an isolating, emotional, relentless and exhausting battle. We are often physically and mentally tired from consistently broken sleep, running around after our children to keep them safe, and the whirlwind of meetings with specialists, appointments, therapies and treatments. In addition to this, we have to navigate a confusing jungle of a system, fighting to make sure our children have access to the services and appointments they need and to make sure that the adults and children they come into contact with accept them and include them. It can be difficult to know where to start or who to turn to for help and advice.

We are our children's greatest advocates and their progress sparks in us intense feelings of joy and pride. Every achievement is a cause for celebration as we appreciate the effort our child has made to get there.

So how can an early years practitioner help?

Practitioners can help by being advocate for our child, just as we are. This is achieved through high-quality teaching that responds to our child's interests, learning styles and needs. It is also achieved by creating an inclusive, nurturing environment in which they are valued.

Like every parent, we want our child to be happy by enjoying a social life with others and by achieving the very best that they can. We want them to have the best possible start in the early years so that they have a chance to live a rewarding and fulfilling life, just as everybody else.

Caring for a child with special educational needs is a journey that parents and practitioners alike navigate through trial and error. That's why we need to listen, learn and work together without judgement. If we all do that we can break down barriers and misconceptions about special educational needs and make sure the child receives an effective, consistent provision so that they can achieve.

The world of special educational needs is a jungle of bureaucracy and confusion which can lead parents to despair. Parents can feel that they have to battle the system in order for their child and the whole family to receive the support they need to achieve a decent quality of life. Caring for a child with special educational needs is challenging for any family. Practitioners can relieve some of the stress on the families by signposting parents towards sources of support, answering their questions knowledgeably, helping them to complete paperwork, listening to their views and collaborating with them to implement practical strategies at home.

The impact of the coronavirus (COVID-19)

Children with SEND have had to manage huge changes to their lives due to the coronavirus lockdown. Following lockdown many will have struggled to settle back into the setting and they might be experiencing ongoing anxiety, behavioural challenges and difficulty separating from a parent or carer. Those entitled to SEN Support and those with EHCPs may not have received some or all of their provision for many months which is likely to have impacted their overall development. Outcomes that children had met prior to lockdown may have had to be revisited.

The coronavirus has impacted different families in different ways and some children will have witnessed confusing situations at home that have arisen from parental stress. Parents who may have been entitled to respite care and short breaks under the Children Act 1989 are unlikely to have received this provision during the pandemic, and with budgets squeezed ever tighter the need will always be greater than the available resource.

During lockdown many parents will have been caring for children with challenging needs without support and for some this has meant providing care through the night too. At the same time they may have had to homeschool siblings, look after babies, and juggle jobs. Many will have been sleep deprived; they may have relationship issues, financial worries, or suffered bereavement. The psychological and emotional effects and the increase in poverty are likely to be felt by children and families for a long time.

Settings can support children with SEND and their families in many ways during this period. In Chapter 1: What is SEND? you will find practical strategies that can be used to support children who may be suffering from anxiety or social and behavioural challenges either as part of an existing condition or as a direct result of the pandemic. Social stories can be effective in explaining difficult social situations to children including the coronavirus - see Chapter 10: Resources and Training, for links.

There are many organisations that offer support to both parents and practitioners to help them to meet the needs of children with SEND and to look after their own wellbeing at the same time. In Chapter 1 you will find organisations listed under conditions and there is a more general list in Chapter 10. Organisations can advise on anything from financial support to helping a child to get a good night's sleep.

In Chapter 2: Legislation, Policies and Procedures we talk about the law surrounding coronavirus and SEND. We help you to keep abreast of developments under the title, 'Coronavirus: keeping up-to-date with legislation'. At the time of writing key legislation such as the Children and Families Act 2014 and the Equality Act 2010 remain in force, but are subject to temporary flexibilities.

In very exceptional circumstances you may have a child on roll who cannot currently attend your setting under the advice of a medical professional. There is no obligation for your setting to provide resources to help them at home but you might decide to do so because you believe the child would benefit. You could put together a pack individually tailored to the child or provide parents with a list of websites where they will find relevant resources. In Chapter 10, there are home learning links specific to early years children with SEND.

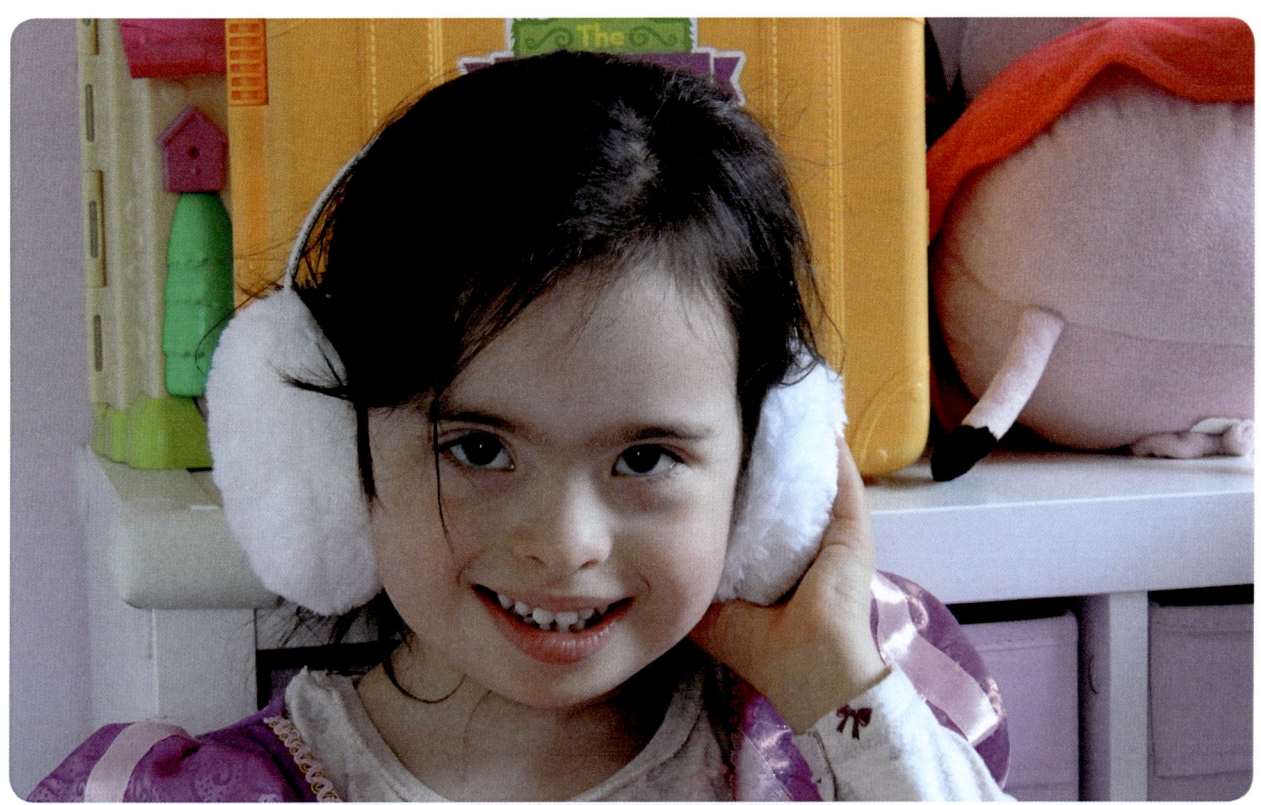

What is SEND?

Children with disabilities do not always have special educational needs (SEN). However, there is significant overlap between these two groups. A child is only defined as having SEN if there is a need for special educational provision to be put in place for them. Under the Children and Families Act 2014 (see Chapter 2) a child is defined as having SEN if they have:

- Greater difficulty in learning than the majority of children the same age, or
- A disability of any kind which hinders them from making full use of mainstream educational facilities without adjustments being made.

In this chapter we give you an overview of the conditions you might come across in your career. The aim is to give you a basic knowledge of each condition, practical ideas to help you to support children with specific conditions, and signposts to further information. Recent research indicates that it is important to look beyond condition labels and to focus upon the skills particular children find difficult. A child with one condition might benefit from the interventions and forms of support described under a different condition. It is vital to be flexible in your approach and to recognise that every child is unique[1].

If you suspect a child has a condition, the first step is to talk to your SENCO who may then organise a meeting with the setting manager and the child's parents to discuss what action to take.

When caring for a child with special educational needs and disability (SEND) it is important to communicate with parents each day. Think about what information you need to share in relation to their child's condition. A parent communication diary (which can be bought or printed online) can be adapted to ensure key information is passed on.

ADHD

Attention Deficit Hyperactivity Disorder (ADHD) is a set of behaviours that impair the ability to control impulsive behaviour and to concentrate. It has also been described as a 'bombardment of the senses' when people become overwhelmed by everyday situations.

What are the signs?

It is not easy to diagnose a child under six with ADHD because impulsive and inattentive behaviours are normal at this stage, but here are some possible indicators:

- Extreme anxiety when separated from parents.
- Poor fine motor skills compared to their peers.
- Struggles to sit still even when engaged in an activity they enjoy.
- Behaves aggressively.
- Difficulty managing emotions.
- Refuses to join in with activities and struggles with certain tasks.
- Hyperactive and impulsive with no awareness of danger.
- Easily distracted, forgetful and with a short attention span – constantly flitting between activities.
- Parents might notice that other parents don't invite their child to social occasions because of poor behaviour.

Take action

Although children are not officially diagnosed in their preschool years, the earlier ADHD is noticed the better for the child. Parental training in behaviour management can make a big difference.

Here are some practical steps you can take:

- Have a strong, predictable routine in place so the child knows what to expect and when.
- Don't overstimulate the child by overwhelming them with experiences, noises, sensations and too many activities.
- Make sure your behavioural policy is strong and consistently applied – communicate with parents so you work together.
- Reduce waiting times for activities and snacks.
- All staff must be calm, consistent and positive in their approach to the child.
- Children with ADHD struggle with group situations that involve waiting, turn-taking and sharing. Anticipate this, and work on specific skills with them.

Further information'

ADHD in the Early Years, Teach Early Years: https://www.teachearlyyears.com/a-unique-child/view/adhd-in-the-early-years
ADHD Foundation: https://www.adhdfoundation.org.uk/

Attention deficit hyperactivity disorder: diagnosis and management, NICE: https://www.nice.org.uk/guidance/ng87

More symptoms of ADHD, NHS: https://www.nhs.uk/conditions/attention-deficit-hyperactivity-disorder-adhd/

The Hyperactive Children's Support Group: http://www.hacsg.org.uk/

Anxiety

We all feel anxious at times, which is perfectly normal. Anxiety is only a problem when it gets in the way of daily life. For children, severe anxiety affects their social and emotional development and is damaging to their self-esteem. There might be a trigger for a child's anxiety such as a change at home or in the setting - any kind of emotional upheaval.

What are the signs?

- Can't focus or settle down to an activity.
- Quick to become angry or irritable.
- Expresses negative thoughts.
- Constantly worries and seeks reassurance from others.
- Fidgety and tense.
- Cries a lot and is clingy.
- Runs away to escape from situations.
- Often complains of sickness and tummy aches.
- Seems tired because they may not be sleeping properly – perhaps they are wetting the bed or having bad dreams.

Take action

Teach children how to manage stress by:

- Sharing and talking about worries using picture books (type 'picture books about anxiety' into a search engine). Use the word 'worries' rather than 'anxieties'.
- Teach mindfulness and yoga techniques – see 'Further Information'.

- Focus on one thing at a time and encourage children to do the same.
- Provide plenty of opportunities for relaxing activities, identifying what the child wants to do (puzzles, stories, singing etc).
- Have designated quiet areas.
- Ensure children eat healthily and take naps if appropriate.
- Provide relaxation activities such as:
  - Painting on enormous pieces of paper with fingers, hands, feet, elbows etc.
  - Paper mache. Ripping paper relieves stress.
  - Physical activity. Active play such as running, jumping and climbing relieve stress.
  - Laughing – laughter is the best medicine! Sing silly songs, share funny stories, and put on ridiculous puppet shows.

Further Information

Anxiety UK: http://www.anxietyuk.org.uk/

Anxiety disorders in children, NHS: https://www.nhs.uk/conditions/anxiety-disorders-in-children/

Anxiety: Management of anxiety (panic disorder, with or without agoraphobia, and generalised anxiety disorder) in adults in primary, secondary and community care, NICE: https://www.nice.org.uk/guidance/CG22

Helping your child with anxiety, Young Minds, https://youngminds.org.uk/find-help/for-parents/parents-guide-to-support-a-z/parents-guide-to-support-anxiety/

The Expert Parent's Guide to Childhood Anxiety, Tutorful: https://tutorful.co.uk/guides/the-expert-guide-to-help-your-child-with-anxiety/how-to-help-children-with-anxiety

Mindful Kids (Mindful Tots) by Whitney Stewart and Mina Braun, Barefoot Books, 2017

Yoga For Kids by Susannah Hoffman and Patricia Arquette, Dorling Kindersley, 2018

Auditory Processing Disorder (APD)

Auditory Processing Disorder (APD) is different from a hearing impairment. In fact, the person can have perfect hearing. Instead it is a failure to process what is being said because the brain can't interpret it.

The child might be able to repeat a message back to you almost exactly, but they don't understand what you have said.

What are the signs?

- Takes an unusually long time to respond to oral communication or doesn't respond.
- Frequently asks for information to be repeated.
- Inappropriate responses to oral communication.
- Difficulty following instructions.
- Difficulty learning songs or nursery rhymes.
- Misunderstands messages.
- Speech and language difficulties.
- General learning difficulties and lack of focus.

Take action

A child with APD will be diagnosed by a speech and language therapist (SLT) who will support the setting. Here's how you can help:

- Make sure it is quiet before you speak to the child.
- When you give an instruction keep it simple.
- Use visual aids where possible.
- Use sequencing words like 'first' and 'second'.
- Encourage eye-contact to aid listening.
- Pause often when you are speaking to give the child a chance to process what you are saying.
- Emphasise key words and slow your speech down.
- Give the child a heads-up when something is about to happen: 'Are you ready?'
- Use visual cues for instructions and to communicate important information.
- Consider using assistive technology such as headphones to reduce background noise, and you can talk to the child through a microphone.

Further information
Auditory Processing Disorder UK:
http://apduk.org.uk/

Auditory processing disorder, NHS:
https://www.nhs.uk/conditions/auditory-processing-disorder/

Autism Spectrum Disorder (ASD)

Autism Spectrum Disorder (ASD) is a developmental, lifelong disability that affects how a person experiences the world around them and how they relate to and communicate with others. Although those with ASD share certain difficulties everyone is affected differently. Some children will have learning disabilities as a result of the condition, whilst others will have mental health or other conditions. Children require different types of support depending upon how and to what degree ASD affects them.

Up until 2013 autism was categorised under separate conditions, with one of those being Asperger's Syndrome. In 2013 a revised version of the 'Diagnostic and Statistical Manual of Mental Disorders (DSM)'[2] was published which combined the different conditions into autism spectrum disorder (ASD). It remains a controversial decision since the vast majority of those with autism have a degree of cognitive impairment, whereas those with Asperger's Syndrome do not.

What are the signs?

Autism tends to be much more difficult to identify in girls than in boys. Susan Epstein, clinical neuropsychologist says, "The model that we have for a classic autism diagnosis has really turned out to be a male model. That's not to say that girls don't ever fit it, but girls tend to have a quieter presentation, with not necessarily as much of the repetitive and restricted behavior, or it shows up in a different way."[3]

Here are some signs to look out for, taking into account the age and developmental stage of a child:

- Dislikes any changes to routine.
- Doesn't respond to their name or smile at you.
- Avoids eye contact.
- Doesn't talk as much as other children.
- Repeats the same phrases (see 'Echolalia').
- Difficulty interpreting both verbal and non-verbal language like facial expressions, tone of voice and abstract concepts.
- Some children with ASD may not speak, or have fairly limited speech. They will often understand more of what other people say to them than they are able to express.

- Unable to listen and concentrate to the same degree as most other children the same age.
- Takes what is said to them literally.
- Over-sensitive or under-sensitive to sounds, tastes, smells, touch, light, colours, temperatures or pain. They may show clear distress over loud noises or have problems with eating and toilet behaviour.
- Seeks out time alone when overwhelmed.
- Repetitive movements, such as flapping their hands, flicking their fingers or rocking their body.
- Obsessive interests to a noticeable degree.
- Difficulty recognising or understanding others' feelings and intentions.
- Struggles to ask others for help and doesn't seek comfort when they are upset.

Take action

- Keep routines clear and consistent.
- Talk to the child in advance of any changes to the usual routine such as a visitor coming to the setting.
- Be explicit and direct in your language so there is less room for misinterpretation.
- Break down instructions, and keep your language simple.
- Give the child more time to process and respond to information.
- Ask questions to check they have understood you.
- Read picture books about autism to all the children so they begin to understand the world from the child's perspective. Type 'picture books about autism syndrome' into a search engine. CBeebies' Pablo is a great series for children to watch together.
- Keep talking to the child to find out how they are feeling and what strategies are working best for them.
- Establish a safe place where the child can go to have some quiet time by themselves.
- Agree with the child an appropriate way they can get attention from you without speaking, eg. by touching you on your arm.
- Use visual cues as much as possible eg. visual timetables, pictorial instructions, posters and labels.
- Share and discuss picture books that enable the child to practise seeing the world from different people's perspectives. Role play and puppet shows can also help the child to learn the social skills that don't come naturally to them.

- Learn about the child's particular sensory needs and adapt the environment to help them. Talk to parents and other professionals who support the child for ideas.
- At meal times accept that the child might use their fingers. If they find sitting with other children too much allow them to sit on their own and gradually introduce other children.
- If the child is fixated on a particular subject use this to help them learn. For example, if they love trains use trains to teach numbers and letters.
- Try to minimize meltdowns by knowing what the child's triggers are. Seek advice from parents and keep a behaviour diary to help identify triggers.

Further information

Ambitious About Autism:
https://www.ambitiousaboutautism.org.uk/

Autism, NHS: https://www.nhs.uk/conditions/autism/

Autism Education Trust:
http://www.autismeducationtrust.org.uk/

Autism Speaks: https://www.autismspeaks.org/pdd-nos

Autistica: http://autistica.org.uk

National Autistic Society: https://www.autism.org.uk/

Teaching young children on the autistic spectrum, National Autistic Society: https://www.autism.org.uk/professionals/teachers/teaching-young-children.aspx

5 symptoms of high-functioning autism, Applied Behavior Analysis Programs Guide: https://www.appliedbehavioranalysisprograms.com/lists/5-symptoms-of-high-functioning-autism/

Asperger's Syndrome

Although Asperger's Syndrome is no longer a separate category under Autistic Spectrum Disorder (ASD), we've decided to keep it separate because it remains a useful term for professionals. That's because children with Asperger's Syndrome do not have a language disorder and/or learning difficulty.

Children with Asperger's Syndrome have problems communicating and interacting socially which means they can struggle to build a rapport with others. They see the world in a different way and that can cause them considerable anxiety.

Further information
Asperger Syndrome UK:
http://www.asperger-syndrome.me.uk/

Behavioural Difficulties: EBD, SEBD, SEMH

Behavioural difficulties are categorised as:

- Emotional behavioural difficulties (EBD)
- Social and emotional behavioural difficulties (SEBD)
- Social, emotional and mental health difficulties (SEMH)

Children with behavioural difficulties display disruptive, antisocial and/or aggressive behaviour which means they have problems developing relationships with others. A child might display disruptive behaviour as a result of a special educational need, but not always. In the early years the most common conditions are:

- Anxiety. This seems surprising because we associate anxiety with drawing in on oneself, but it can lead to temper tantrums and meltdowns too.
- Autism Spectrum Disorder (ASD)
- Attention Deficit Hyperactivity Disorder (ADHD)
- Oppositional Defiant Disorder.

We talk about most of these conditions separately in this chapter.

Take action

Do your best to reduce incidences of poor behaviour by learning as much as you can about the underlying condition and by understanding what is likely to trigger challenging behaviour.

If a child has an EHCP, behavioural strategies will have been agreed and must be consistently followed. For children whose condition is not yet diagnosed an IBP (Individual Behavioural Plan) can be put in place by the SENCO in partnership with other professionals and with the involvement of parents. At the IBP meeting the child's triggers will be discussed and behavioural strategies will be agreed. The IBP should follow the graduated approach strategy – assess, plan, do, review to make sure it remains effective.

Share your experiences with parents, the SENCO and other professionals involved with the child so that together you can find and apply strategies which are more likely to work. Managing challenging behaviour is stressful especially as what works one day may not work the next. Behaviour management is a team effort.

Some local authorities have published behaviour support guidance and IBP proformas online for practitioners to use.

In Ofsted's new education inspection framework, bullying and discrimination are covered under the heading 'Behaviour and Attitudes'. There is a great emphasis on how effectively and quickly providers take action when incidents occur. Inspectors might base their judgements upon what children tell them and what they observe in the setting rather than what managers and SENCOs say they are doing.[4]

Further information
EYFS Guidance - Challenging Behaviour: what can I do to help, New River College: http://newrivercollege.co.uk/wp-content/uploads/2015/10/EYFS-PSP-and-guidance.pdf

Great Ormond Street, Department of Child and Adolescent Mental Health: https://www.gosh.nhs.uk/medical-information/clinical-specialties/department-child-and-adolescent-mental-health-dcamh-0

NHS: Antisocial Personality Disorder: https://www.nhs.uk/conditions/antisocial-personality-disorder/

Promoting the social and emotional wellbeing of children and young people, SEBD: https://www.sebda.org/sebd/

The Challenging Behaviour Foundation: https://www.challengingbehaviour.org.uk/supporting-you/for-professionals/booklist.html

What is Conduct Disorder? https://www.healthline.com/health/conduct-disorder

Down Syndrome

Down Syndrome is a chromosomal condition caused by the presence of an extra chromosome (chromosome 21) in the cells. This additional genetic material results in a range of physical and developmental characteristics. There are three types of Down Syndrome:

- Trisomy 21. This is the most common type, where there are three number 21 chromosomes in every cell of the body instead of two.
- Translocation. Part of chromosome 21 breaks off at the time of cell division and attaches to another chromosome.
- Mosaicism. When some cells have two copies of chromosome 21 (like everybody else), but some cells have three. This is the rarest form of Down Syndrome.

Children with Down Syndrome develop at their own pace and have strengths and weaknesses associated with the condition. They have Global Developmental Delay (see below) and some behavioural difficulties. The main areas of delay are caused by speech and language difficulties, auditory short-term memory and processing skills, short concentration span, hearing loss due to glue ear, and visual conditions.

Physically, they have delayed fine and gross motor skills due to low muscle tone (hypotonia) and hypermobility (see 'Joint Hypermobility Syndrome' below). Some children with Down Syndrome also have other medical conditions and may have a dual diagnosis of autism and ADHD.

Take action

If you believe a child can succeed and you have a positive, encouraging attitude towards them they will fulfill their potential and will very likely exceed your expectations.

Here we outline some general ways you can support a child with Down Syndrome, but it is important that your approach is tailored to a particular child as agreed with fellow professionals, and the child's parents.

- Children with Down Syndrome are visual learners and learn by reinforcement and repetition so teach new skills through demonstration rather than verbal instruction alone. Always check back to ensure that the skills have been learnt.
- Use communication systems to support the child, such as a sign language, timetables and PECS for routines, instructions and transitions. Make sure there's sharing and consistency between the setting and the child's home. Peers can learn sign language so they can communicate and socialise with the child. See 'Speech and Language Difficulties'.
- Before explaining an activity make sure the child is looking at you first. Ensure face-to-face and direct eye contact. Give the child time to process the information.
- Use simple, familiar language and short sentences. For transitions use words such as 'first' and 'then'.
- Children might be oversensitive or undersensitive to textures, tastes, sounds and colours/lights so you need to adapt activities and the environment to support them.
- Encourage language development and fine motor skills through sensory activities. Use bright colours, different materials, messy play, play dough, puppets and books (especially those with sounds).
- Keep routines clear and consistent using visual cues such as photographs, symbols and objects of reference. Give enough time for the child to prepare for transitions throughout the day eg. storytime or outside play.

- Children with Down Syndrome respond well to praise and rewards. Reinforce positive behaviour immediately with visual, and oral rewards.
- Provide lots of opportunities for outdoor play and playing with their peers. The child might need help to ask to join in and need adult prompting and guidance to participate.
- Inform parents if there is any outbreak of illness in the setting because children with Down Syndrome have a low immune system making them more susceptible.

Further information

Down's Syndrome Association: https://www.downs-syndrome.org.uk/for-new-parents/education/early-years/

Down's Syndrome, Mencap: https://www.mencap.org.uk/learning-disability-explained/conditions/downs-syndrome?gclid=CjwKCAjw7O_pBRA3EiwA_lmtfjJ-zaSVotyPahLcRUqkt9QMYNsNeeRsNnHgpmQl0S3rHRLHgzR-nRoC-vwQAvD_BwE

Down's Syndrome (Trisomy 21), Stanford Children's Health: https://www.stanfordchildrens.org/en/topic/default?id=down-syndrome-trisomy-21-90-P02356

Including children with Down's Syndrome in Early Childhood Care and Education Settings, Down Syndrome Ireland: https://downsyndrome.ie/wp-content/uploads/2018/03/Including-Children-Early-Education-1.pdf

Mosaic Down's Syndrome.com: http://www.mosaicdownsyndrome.com/

Translocation Down's Syndrome, Stanford Children's Health: https://www.stanfordchildrens.org/en/topic/default?id=translocation-down-syndrome-90-P02153

Dyscalculia

People with dyscalculia have difficulty with numeracy and mathematical concepts. It's a condition often defined as 'number blindness'.

Dyscalculia isn't diagnosed until the age of seven because it's difficult to clearly distinguish between dyscalculia and other developmental delays before that age.

Further information

How to spot dyscalculia, Child Mind Institute: https://childmind.org/article/how-to-spot-dyscalculia/

For Learning and Attention Issues, Understood: https://www.understood.org/en/learning-attention-issues/child-learning-disabilities/dyscalculia/dyscalculia-what-youre-seeing-in-your-preschooler

Unlocking Learning Ability, Davis Facilitators: https://www.unlocking-learning.co.uk/dyscalculia-in-the-early-years/

Dyslexia

Dyslexia is a lifelong condition which causes difficulties with specific learning abilities such as reading, writing, spelling, sequencing, short-term memory, motor skills, auditory perception, and visual perception. Dyslexia may range from mild to severe and the difficulties can occur at any level of intellectual development.

Further information

Is my child dyslexic? British Dylexia Association https://www.bdadyslexia.org.uk/advice/children/is-my-child-dyslexic/signs-of-dyslexia-early-years

https://www.nhs.uk/conditions/dyslexia/

NICE https://www.evidence.nhs.uk/search?q=dyslexia

Dyspraxia

Dyspraxia, also known as Developmental Coordination Disorder (DCD) affects people's fine and/or gross motor coordination. For most people with the condition there is no identified cause. Recent research suggests that it may be caused by an immaturity of brain neuron development and not brain damage.

What are the signs?

When noticing signs, take into account the child's developmental stage comparing them with the majority of their peers and assessing them against the Early Years Outcomes.

- Delay in reaching milestones such as speaking, walking, standing, sitting and rolling over, jumping, hopping or catching a ball.
- Finds it hard to walk up and down stairs.
- Falls over more than most children.
- Struggles to get dressed and undressed.
- Is slow to complete everyday tasks involving fine or gross motor skills.
- Has poor pencil grip and immature artwork.
- Finds it difficult to focus and is easily distracted and anxious.
- Finds jigsaws or sorting games very difficult.

Take Action

You will follow the advice of their occupational therapist and/or a physiotherapist. The action you take will depend upon the nature of the child's coordination difficulties. If they are delayed in meeting gross motor difficulties then you might practise throwing and catching different sized balls with them, or balancing on different types of surfaces.

If they have trouble dressing themselves they could practise dressing by sitting down with their back against the wall for support.

The Dyspraxia Foundation – Early Years Guidelines, provides a range of strategies you can employ to address specific needs.

Further Information
Developmental coordination disorder (dyspraxia) in children NHS: https://www.nhs.uk/conditions/developmental-coordination-disorder-dyspraxia/symptoms/

Dyspraxia Association: https://dyspraxiafoundation.org.uk

Early Years Guidelines, Dyspraxia Foundation: https://dyspraxiafoundation.org.uk/wp-content/uploads/2014/12/Early-Years-Guidelines.pdf

Echolalia

This is a speech and language disorder where a child repeats what you say. If you ask the child, 'Would you like a biscuit?' the child will say 'biscuit' instead of 'yes'. There is also a type of echolalia called 'delayed echolalia' when a child repeats something they have heard in the past. For instance they may randomly repeat a line from a favourite film.

Up until the age of one, echolalia is part of normal development. However, by the age of three echolalia should be minimal and children should be communicating in their own words.

Delayed echolalia, like repeating lines from films, is normal now and again, but you will instinctively feel something is unusual if a child seems to be repeating the same thing over and over again.

Echolalia can indicate autism or delayed language skills, so it is important to diagnose it early.

Take action

Refer the child to a speech and language therapist who will tailor strategies to meet the child's specific needs.

Further information
Echolalia, Healthline: https://www.healthline.com/health/echolalia

Echolalia: when children repeat what you say, Speech and Language Kids: https://www.speechandlanguagekids.com/echolalia-when-children-repeat-what-you-say/

Global Developmental Delay (GDD)/Developmental Delay

If a child fails to reach two or more early years foundation stage milestones they may have Global Developmental Delay (GDD) which is also known as 'Developmental Delay'. A child might have a short-term delay which may not require any intervention at all or may be overcome with a period of additional support, or they might have a long-term learning disability.

Children with long-term learning disabilities may have an acute intellectual impairment and their physical, emotional, social and/or sensory development may be affected. Their needs may be complex and significant, requiring a high level of adult support, and they may also have medical conditions.

What are the signs?

You will notice a child who isn't meeting the milestones through your ongoing assessments and observations.

Here are some signs to look for in a child under a year old:

- Underdeveloped fine and gross motor skills.
- Unable to sit upright by 8 months.
- Cannot crawl by 11 months.
- Not walking by 18 months.
- Not making babbling sounds by 4 months.

For children over a year old, signs could include delay in meeting the following milestones:

- Speech and language. The child's ability to communicate. 'Speech' refers to understanding and using verbal language. 'Language' includes both verbal and non-verbal communication – gestures and body language as well as spoken language.
- Cognitive. This refers to thinking and conscious mental processes. It affects the child's ability to concentrate, memorise and learn new skills.

- Social and emotional. Poor social and emotional skills can lead to poor behaviour, learning difficulties, difficulties making friends as well as psychiatric disorders.
- Gross and fine motor skills. Noticeably poorer fine and gross motor skills than their peers.

Just because a child has failed to reach a milestone on time does not necessarily mean you need to intervene. Children develop at different speeds and many will catch-up naturally. It is a question of remaining vigilant and keeping lines of communication open with the SENCO and the child's parents.

Take action

The action you take will depend upon the nature and severity of the child's needs. Refer to the 'Take action' sections for the other conditions in this chapter and the websites listed below. Also see Chapter 3: SEN Support and Chapter 7: Removing Barriers to Learning.

Further information

A Know How Guide - The EYFS progress check at age 2: https://www.foundationyears.org.uk/files/2012/03/A-Know-How-Guide.pdf

Early years guide to the 0-25 SEND code of practice: https://assets.publishing.service.gov.uk/government/uploads/system/uploads/attachment_data/file/350685/Early_Years_Guide_to_SEND_Code_of_Practice_-_02Sept14.pdf

Early identification of special needs, Council for Disabled Children: https://www.foundationyears.org.uk/files/2015/06/Section-4-First-concerns-and-early-identification.pdf

Global developmental delay, Mencap, https://www.mencap.org.uk/learning-disability-explained/conditions/global-development-delay

Global developmental delay, Contact: https://contact.org.uk/advice-and-support/medical-information/conditions/g/global-developmental-delay/

Learning disabilities, NHS: https://www.nhs.uk/conditions/learning-disabilities/

Making Play Inclusive, Sense. Type 'making play inclusive Sense' into a search engine to locate the PDF file on their website (which is http://www.sense.org.uk)

Mencap (search 'global developmental delay'): https://www.mencap.org.uk/

The child with general learning disability: for parents and carers, Royal College of Psychiatrists: https://www.rcpsych.ac.uk/mental-health/parents-and-young-people/information-for-parents-and-carers/the-child-with-general-learning-disability-for-parents-and-carers

Hearing Impairment and Deafness

'Hearing impairment' covers a spectrum from mild to profound hearing loss. 'Deafness' refers to complete hearing loss. Hearing loss can be temporary, such as glue ear (see the table below under 'Physical Conditions'), long-term or permanent.

There are lots of reasons why a child is deaf or hearing impaired. It is thought that permanent deafness is passed

on in the genes, even though nobody else in the child's family might be deaf. Sometimes deafness or a hearing impairment is the result of an illness, but sometimes the cause cannot be identified.

What are the signs?

- The child doesn't respond when called.
- They need the volume turned up on the television.
- They mishear what you say.
- They mispronounce words.
- There is delayed speech and language development.
- They seem tired, frustrated or have difficulty concentrating.
- Babies can pull their ears or have red ears.

Take action

If you suspect a child has a hearing difficulty tell the parents who will then need to book an appointment to see the doctor. The doctor will refer the child to an audiologist.

What else you can do:

- Work with parents, the health visitor, speech and language therapists, and the child's audiologist to ensure the child can access the curriculum.
- Use their hearing technology or language system effectively, eg. Makaton or BSL.
- Face the child when you speak to them so they can see your face.
- Speak clearly but don't shout.
- Interact with them in small, focused groups or one-to-one.
- Use visual aids, such as objects of reference.
- Check that the child has understood you by asking questions.
- Reduce the background noise as much as possible thinking about noisy equipment and having carpets instead of hard floors. Put noisy equipment, such as building blocks, on a clothed surface to reduce noise.
- When talking in a bigger group, sit the child near the front.
- Keep to a specific routine, as this helps the child to learn language by hearing it over and over again. Share familiar stories that repeat sentences, and play games that require the child to follow the same pattern.
- Don't tire them out. Make sure they have breaks between activities.

Further Information
Action on Hearing Loss: http://actiononhearingloss.org.uk

Hearing loss, NHS:
https://www.nhs.uk/conditions/hearing-loss/

National Deaf Children's Society:
https://www.ndcs.org.uk/documents-and-resources/
supporting-the-achievement-of-hearing-impaired-
children-in-early-years-settings/

Advice for Joint Hypermobility in Children, NHS
Greater Glasgow and Clyde:
https://www.nhsggc.org.uk/kids/resources/health-a-z-
resources/advice-for-joint-hypermobility-in-children/

An Educator's Guide: Meeting the Needs of an Ehlers-
Danlos child: https://ehlers-danlos.com/wp-content/
uploads/Educator-Parent-Guide-2016.pdf
Joint hypermobility syndrome, NHS: https://www.nhs.uk/
conditions/joint-hypermobility-syndrome/

Joint Hypermobility Syndrome

Joint hypermobility means that a person can move some or all of their joints more than most people can. Joint hypermobility isn't a medical condition in itself – many people don't realise they are hypermobile if it doesn't cause them any problems. When it causes pain it or dislocation it might be Joint Hypermobility Syndrome or Ehlers-Danlos syndromes (EDS).

What are the signs?

- Muscle pain or strain when they move their joints.
- Joint stiffness which might be caused by fluid collecting inside the joint.
- Foot and ankle pain particularly after standing for a long time. The child's ankles may easily twist.
- Neck pain and backache.
- Dislocated or injured joints.
- Tiredness because they are working hard to maintain physical positions due to laxity in their joints.
- Fine and gross motor skill difficulties.
- Lack of awareness of where their joints are in space without having to look.

Take action

Speak to the child's parent for a referral to a physiotherapist and orthotist. Oxleas NHS, 'Advice for hypermobility' gives practical advice. Also see 'Motor Skills Difficulties' and 'Dyspraxia' for helpful strategies.

Further Information
Advice for hypermobility, Oxleas NHS:
http://oxleas.nhs.uk/site-media/cms-downloads/Advice_
for_hypermobility_May_2014.pdf

Motor Skills Difficulties

A child may have difficulties with their fine motor skills, gross motor skills, or both. Fine motor skills refer to small muscle movements involving effective use of hands and fingers. Gross motor skills relate to the large muscles of the legs, arms and torso. Also see 'Dyspraxia'.

What are the signs?

Children with fine motor difficulties may struggle to use cutlery, build with lego, thread beads, fasten buttons etc. Those with gross motor skills might have difficulty standing, sitting, walking, running, jumping and so on. Their skills will seem underdeveloped compared to their peers and they will fail to reach EYFS goals.

Take action

If a child is unable to perform a specific age-appropriate skill like using scissors, it might be nothing to worry about. Perhaps it's due to lack of practice? You could encourage the child to engage in scissor-based activities by incorporating scissors into their interests. For instance, if the child likes cars, they could make a cardboard box garage for their cars.

However, if the child has multiple fine or gross motor difficulties they will need additional help. They may need support from physiotherapists or occupational therapists who will advise on activities and exercises for the child and ways in which you can differentiate daily activities.

The VeryWell Family and NHS websites are packed with gross and fine motor activities children can do at home with parents and in the setting.

Further Information

Fine motor skills information for schools, NHS: https://www.swft.nhs.uk/our-services/children-and-young-peoples-services/occupational-therapy/fine-motor-skills-information-schools

Gross Motor Skills Activities for Little Kids, VeryWell Family: https://www.verywellfamily.com/gross-motor-skills-for-preschoolers-1257160

Obsessive Compulsive Disorder (OCD)

Obsessive compulsive disorder (OCD) is often linked to anxiety. It is when somebody has compulsive behaviour or obsessive thoughts.

What are the signs?

- Obsessive washing due to fear of germs or dirt.
- Needing order, precision and symmetry.
- Preoccupation with bodily wastes.
- Terror of becoming ill or death (themselves and those they love).

- Going back time and time again to check something is done properly.
- Seeking constant reassurance that they are performing a task correctly.

Take action

Talk to the child's parents about their experiences with the child and together with them put strategies in place to help the child. They could contact their health visitor or GP for further advice. You might need to make adaptations to the environment or take extra time to boost the child's self-esteem and confidence. See 'Anxiety'.

Further information

How to help your child, Obsessive Compulsive Foundation of Metropolitan Chicago: https://adaa.org/sites/default/files/How-to-Help-Your-Child-A-Parents-Guide-to-OCD.pdf

Obsessive compulsive disorder, NHS: https://www.nhs.uk/conditions/obsessive-compulsive-disorder-ocd/

OCD Action: https://www.ocdaction.org.uk/

OCD UK: http://www.ocduk.org/ocd/

Oppositional Defiant Disorder (ODD)

Oppositional Defiant Disorder (ODD) is a psychiatric condition which affects a child's behaviour. The child will be aggressive towards others. ODD is not diagnosed in children under the age of three because it is normal to have temper tantrums at this age. After the age of three children are capable of expressing themselves verbally and they begin to understand socially acceptable behaviour.

What are the signs?

To be diagnosed with ODD the child must have displayed defiant behaviour for at least six months. ODD behaviour includes:

- Deliberately trying to upset others.
- Frequent temper tantrums.

- Argumentative.
- Defiant towards authority.
- Resenting others and often blaming them.
- Being oversensitive.
- Lying and stealing.

It's difficult to say what causes ODD, but factors may include a lack of confidence and self-esteem or a traumatic life experience. There is some overlap between ODD and ADHD.

Take action

If it is appropriate, parents need to be asked to contact their health visitor or GP who might refer the child to the NHS mental health support services team (CAMHS). You could also contact the social worker linked to your setting for advice.

Support the child in the setting by:

- Working in partnership with parents to ensure consistent, effective behaviour management strategies.
- Identifying what triggers the child's unwanted behaviour by keeping a diary.
- Putting a robust, consistent behaviour management plan in place (IBP)
- Helping the child to feel secure by making sure rules, behaviour expectations and consequences are clear and consistent.
- Providing as much structure as you can through planned activities.
- Helping the child to know what to expect by sharing the timetable and warning them in advance of any changes to the daily routine.
- Using positive reinforcement – praise and reward achievement.
- Not raising your voice. Stay calm and neutral.

Further information
New guidelines on child antisocial behaviour, NHS: https://www.nhs.uk/news/pregnancy-and-child/new-guidelines-on-child-antisocial-behaviour/

Oppositional defiant disorder, Child Mind Institute: https://childmind.org/guide/oppositional-defiant-disorder/

Oppositional defiant disorder, Contact: https://contact.org.uk/advice-and-support/medical-information/conditions/c/conduct-disorder-and-oppositional-defiant-disorder/

Pathological Demand Avoidance (PDA)

Pathological Demand Avoidance (PDA) is an autistic spectrum condition in which children avoid carrying out ordinary requests. They will often say 'no' to something even if it's something they enjoy. Their behaviour is driven by anxiety – a bit like a panic attack. If saying 'no' doesn't work, they might make excuses, try distraction techniques, negotiate, attempt to charm their way out of it, use delaying tactics, shout or throw a tantrum.

What are the signs?

- Doing everything they can to avoid complying with demands.
- Struggles to understand the social hierarchy - they don't respect authority.
- They need to be in control so they order their peers around.
- Highly skilled at pretend play, becoming so engrossed that they confuse pretend and reality.

Take action

- Put a robust, consistent behaviour management plan in place.
- Adjust activities according to what the child's anxiety levels can tolerate on that particular day.
- Work collaboratively with the child rather than being the boss.
- Give instructions indirectly 'I wonder if somebody might be able to help me to tidy the Lego?'
- Make a safe place where the child can go to calm down or be by themselves when they feel overwhelmed.
- When the child is angry, talk to them calmly, quietly and reassuringly.

Further information
Pathological demand avoidance syndrome, Contact: https://contact.org.uk/advice-and-support/medical-information/conditions/p/pathological-demand-avoidance-syndrome/

Pathological Demand Avoidance Society: https://www.pdasociety.org.uk/resources/leaflets

What is pathological demand avoidance (PDA)? National Autistic Society: https://www.autism.org.uk/about/what-is/pda.aspx

Profound and Multiple Learning Disabilities

Profound and Multiple Learning Disabilities (PMLD) is an umbrella term used to describe someone who had multiple and severe disabilities as a result of their condition or conditions. Every child under this category will have an EHCP – see Chapter 5.

Further information
PMLD Link: http://www.pmldlink.org.uk/

Profound and multiple learning disabilities (PMLD), Mencap: https://www.mencap.org.uk/advice-and-support/profound-and-multiple-learning-disabilities-pmld

Sensory Processing Disorder (SPD)

Sensory Processing Disorder (SPD) is also known as Sensory Integration Disorder (SID). It's a condition which affects how the brain receives and interprets sensory information. A child with this condition will have difficulty responding to sensory stimulation. Most children on the autistic spectrum may have SPD.

What are the signs?

They might be oversensitive or undersensitive to:

- Loud noises.
- Smells.
- Light and colour.
- Certain textures.
- The feel of their clothes.
- Another person's touch.
- Food around their mouth.
- Movement and body position.

Oversensitivity and undersensitivity to certain sensations might cause the child to avoid the sensations that repel them, or seek out the sensations that they are not sensitive enough to. The child might chew inedible items, fidget or engage in repetitive movements. Children with SPD also display lack of coordination and bump into things (also see Dyspraxia). They might not be able to tell where their arms and legs are in a space, and they might be difficult to engage in play or conversations.

Children's sensitivity to sensations can vary from day-to-day.

Take action

Your strategies will vary considerably depending upon the child's specific sensory processing issues. Leicestershire NHS Trust's Sensory Processing Resource Pack: Early Years (p.11) gives tailored, practical ways you can help. For example, if the child avoids holding hands with others you can, 'Use a no-pressure approach and allow the child to watch from a distance when their peers are taking part in hand holding games'.

Further information
Sensory processing difficulties, Sheffield Children's NHS: https://www.sheffieldchildrens.nhs.uk/services/child-development-and-neurodisability/sensory-processing-difficulties/

Sensory Processing Disorder, WebMD: https://www.webmd.com/children/sensory-processing-disorder#1

Sensory Processing Resource Pack: Early Years, Leicestershire NHS Trust - http://www.aettraininghubs.org.uk/wp-content/uploads/2014/05/10.2EY-sensory-processing-profile-Leics.pdf

Understanding sensory processing issues, Understood: https://www.understood.org/en/learning-attention-issues/child-learning-disabilities/sensory-processing-issues/understanding-sensory-processing-issues

Social Communication Disorder

This is a diagnosis that might be given where a child displays the social and communication difficulties associated with autism, but doesn't have any other symptoms of autism.

Children will display difficulties with both verbal and non-verbal communication, including sign language. This means that they will also give inappropriate responses in conversations.

What are the signs?

- The child understands many communication and language skills, but cannot apply them in the context of specific social situations.
- There is a delay in reaching language milestones and in social interactions.
- The child doesn't seem to understand what is being said to them, and they show this by responding inappropriately.

Take action

Follow the same strategies as you would for a child with a speech, language and communication disorder.

Further information

Afasic, https://www.afasic.org.uk/

How can I help my child's speech and language development, I Can, https://ican.org.uk/

Social communication disorder basics, Child Mind Institute, https://childmind.org/guide/social-communication-disorder/

Understanding communication disorder, Understood, https://www.understood.org/en/learning-thinking-differences/child-learning-disabilities/communication-disorders/understanding-social-communication-disorder

Speech and Language Difficulties

Most children can understand what is being said to them before they begin to talk. As their communication skills develop they learn to put their feelings and observations into words. As you have been reading this chapter you will have noticed that there are many conditions that can lead to speech and language difficulties.

There are two types of speech and language disorders:

- Receptive language disorder. The child has difficulty understanding the words they hear.
- Expressive language disorder. The child has difficulty or cannot express themselves very clearly through language.

What are the signs?

The signs of a receptive language disorder are difficulties with:

- Understanding what people say and interpreting gestures.
- Understanding what they read.
- Answering questions.
- Grasping concepts.
- Following instructions.
- Identifying objects.

Children with an expressive language disorder may not be able to:

- Use words in the right context.
- Express their thoughts and ideas.
- Tell stories or sing songs.
- Name objects.
- Ask questions.
- Use gestures.

If they are not addressed, speech and language difficulties have a negative impact on every aspect of a child's development.

Speech and language therapists also support children with feeding and swallowing difficulties (dysphagia). They provide direct intervention when children have complex needs and they help parents to manage mealtimes safely.

Take action

Once you have identified that a child has a possible speech and language difficulty you will need to speak to the parents and they will contact the health visitor or GP who could make a referral to a speech and language therapist (SLT)

Some local NHS Trusts offer a speech and language drop-in service for parents. Find information about these by contacting your local child and family centre. More information can be found on your local authority's 'local offer' webpage.

The speech and language therapist will work with you to put a plan in place for the child. Here are some useful strategies:

- Use visual aids to help the child follow routines and learn new words or concepts.
- Label resources with photographs or pictures.
- Provide pictures of activities so the child can point to what they want to do.
- When using verbal instructions, keep them simple and check the child has understood you.
- Demonstrate activities before the child begins, and provide a visual sequence of steps and the outcome you want them to achieve.
- Empower the child to express themselves by using Makaton or another sign language system.
- When addressing the child, get their attention first by looking at them and saying their name. Wait for them to look at you before you speak.
- Simplify your language and slow down your speech when communicating with the child.
- Ask the child fewer questions and emphasise the most important words in the sentence.
- Give the child time to think before they respond to a question.
- When the child makes mistakes, model language by repeating what they have said back to you in the correct way.
- Don't overtly correct them or you may damage their self-confidence, making them afraid to speak for fear of being wrong.
- Use repetitive, simple language for familiar situations and activities.
- As you join in with the child's play, talk to them. Comment on what they are doing and engage in conversation.
- Ask parents if the child has any special words or gestures they use for specific objects to avoid confusion and foster feelings of confidence and security.
- Praise listening skills and attention. Your positive words will encourage them to keep trying!

Further information

Inclusion Development Programme: Speech and Language, Department for Children, Schools and Families, 2008: https://contact.org.uk/advice-and-support/medical-information/conditions/s/speech-and-language-impairment/

Speech or language impairments, Project IDEAL: http://www.projectidealonline.org/v/speech-language-impairments/

Talking Point: http://www.talkingpoint.org.uk/

Visual Impairment (including Duane Syndrome)

A visual impairment is when a part of the eye or the brain that is needed to process images doesn't work properly. A visual impairment cannot be corrected with glasses. It can be caused by a problem with the signal that carries light from the eye to the brain. The brain is unable to interpret the signal. Duane Syndrome is a type of visual impairment that affects the movement of the eye causing sight loss.

A visual impairment will have a varied impact on the child's ability to learn because it depends upon the severity of the condition. The child's parents will need to see their GP rather than an optician if the child is under the age of four. The GP may refer the child to an ophthalmologist

What are the signs?

- Looking cross-eyed, having a 'lazy eye' or a squint.
- Holding books and objects close up to the face.
- Rubbing eyes.
- Tilting the head or covering one eye to see things close up.
- Having accidents or appearing clumsy.

Take action

- Communicate with gentle, physical contact.
- Build the child's self-confidence by providing activities that utilise their skills rather than highlighting their visual difficulty.

- Communicate one-to-one rather than in a large group.
- Make sure the child knows what activities and resources are available for them to play with.
- Adapt resources by, for example, using a large font or bigger equipment.
- Use contrasting surfaces to make things more visible, eg. white sand in a dark tray, or a dark cloth on the snack table so the cup shows up. Black on white or yellow is easier to see than other colours.
- Provide a range of tactile and sensory experiences to support vision.
- Reduce visual clutter in the environment.
- Keep the floor area between activities clear to reduce obstacles.
- Adapt the physical environment as appropriate by changing table surfaces or using lamps.
- If the child will need to use braille later on, then provide activities that will build finger strength.
- Support the child by understanding how their visual impairment has limited their life experiences. For instance, the child may find it difficult to engage in role play activities which draw upon real life scenarios.

Further information

Blindness and vision loss, NHS: https://www.nhs.uk/conditions/vision-loss/

Duane Syndrome, WebMD: https://www.webmd.com/eye-health/duane-syndrome-facts#1

Early Years, RNIB: https://www.rnib.org.uk/information-everyday-living-education-and-learning-young-childrens-education/early-years

SeeAbility: https://www.seeability.org/

Visual Processing Disorder

Visual Processing Disorder (VPD) is different from Visual Impairment because visual input is transmitted to the brain properly, however the brain cannot interpret it.

What are the signs?

The following signs could mean the child has VDP, but they could also indicate dyspraxia, ADHD or dyslexia (although dyslexia is not diagnosed in the early years):

- Inability to focus because they're distracted by other visual stimulus around them. The child is unable to follow instructions or concentrate on an activity as long as their peers.
- The child might bump into furniture, knock over drinks or have frequent accidents because they don't know how near or far away objects are from them.
- A child who is beginning to read will have difficulty distinguishing between similar letters or symbols.

Take action

- Narrate and describe visuals for the child.
- Provide access to audio stories.
- Set out a range of multi-sensory resources and activities, encouraging the child to describe what they feel to extend their vocabulary.
- Help the child to develop visual processing skills by:
  - Doing puzzles together.
  - Playing ball games.
  - Choosing picture books which require them to look at fine details. For example in Bob's Best Ever Friend by Simon Bartram, children search for a hidden alien dog on each page.
  - Playing memory games such as matching pairs.

Further information

Classroom accommodations for visual processing issues, Understood: https://www.understood.org/en/school-learning/partnering-with-childs-school/instructional-strategies/at-a-glance-classroom-accommodations-for-visual-processing-issues

What is visual processing disorder? Churchill Center and School: https://www.churchillstl.org/learning-disability-resources/visual-processing-disorder/

Physical Conditions

A child with a medical condition might need to have an individual healthcare plan put in place for them. This is separate from an education, health and care plan (EHCP) which we talk about in Chapter 5.

An individual healthcare plan is necessary if a child has a complex or severe medical condition. Common conditions that require healthcare plans are allergies, asthma, continence issues, diabetes and epilepsy. An individual healthcare plan is designed to keep a child safe.

Visit the following links for more information about individual healthcare plans:

Supporting pupils with medical conditions in school, gov.uk: https://assets.publishing.service.gov.uk/government/uploads/system/uploads/attachment_data/file/803956/supporting-pupils-at-school-with-medical-conditions.pdf

The SchoolRun.com, Individual Healthcare Plans: https://www.theschoolrun.com/school-individual-healthcare-plans

In the opposite page there is a summary of conditions you might come across in mainstream education and where to find more information.

Condition	Educational implications	Further information
Asthma	Asthma is a disease of the lungs which causes breathing difficulties. Children might miss out on education due to illnesses such as chest infections. When asthma isn't properly controlled by medication it can cause depression and tiredness.	Asthma UK: https://www.asthma.org.uk/ NHS: https://www.nhs.uk/conditions/asthma/
Cerebral palsy	Cerebral palsy affects movement, coordination, and balance. The symptoms of cerebral palsy appear in the first three years of a child's life. Depending upon the severity, some children will be able to attend a mainstream setting.	Cerebral Palsy UK: https://www.cerebralpalsy.org.uk/ ITV's This Morning lists Cerebral palsy helplines: https://www.itv.com/thismorning/cerebral-palsy-helplines NHS: https://www.nhs.uk/conditions/cerebral-palsy/
Incontinence	Incontinence is an embarrassing issue in which someone has bowel or bladder control issues. The condition can damage their self-esteem leading to mental health disorders.	NICE: https://www.nice.org.uk/search?q=children%20continence The Children's Bowel and Bladder Charity: https://www.eric.org.uk/childrens-continence-pathway
Cystic fibrosis	Cystic fibrosis affects the respiratory, digestive and reproductive organs. Digestive system problems mean that children have trouble getting nutrients into their bodies. This can result in concentration difficulties and an inability to engage in learning.	Cystic Fibrosis Trust: https://www.cysticfibrosis.org.uk/ NHS: https://www.nhs.uk/conditions/cystic-fibrosis/
Diabetes	Type 1 diabetes occurs when the pancreas cannot produce insulin causing high blood sugar levels. Children can have difficulties with attention, memory and perceptual processing skills, if their diabetes is not managed.	Diabetes UK: https://www.diabetes.org.uk/guide-to-diabetes/your-child-and-diabetes/schools/school-staff NHS: https://www.nhs.uk/conditions/diabetes/
Eating and drinking difficulties	Some children with special educational needs and disability may have difficulty eating and drinking. This might be as a result of a condition such as cerebral palsy, Down's syndrome or autism. A speech and language therapist and also a dietician (if the child is underweight) may be involved in their care.	Eating difficulties, Scope: https://www.scope.org.uk/advice-and-support/a-z-eating-difficulties/ Food fact sheets, The Association of UK Dieticians: https://www.bda.uk.com/
Epilepsy	For some children, epilepsy has no impact on their education, but others suffer learning and/or behavioural difficulties. Epileptic seizures can damage memory and interrupt a child's sleep making it difficult for them to learn. The medicines children take can also have side effects including hyperactivity, irritability, aggression, drowsiness, dizziness, memory difficulties, trouble concentrating and mood swings.	Epilepsy Action: https://www.epilepsy.org.uk/info/education/learning-and-behaviour Epilepsy Society: https://www.epilepsysociety.org.uk/ NHS: https://www.nhs.uk/conditions/epilepsy/
Fragile X syndrome	People with this genetic condition suffer from learning difficulties – boys are more severely affected than girls. They can have short attention spans, be impulsive and restless. In social situations they may act in a similar way to those with autism.	Fragile X Society: https://www.fragilex.org.uk/ Genetic Alliance: https://www.geneticalliance.org.uk/
Glue ear	Glue ear is normally a temporary illness whereby the ear fills with fluid. In some cases it is long-term, which can impact children's speech and language development. Children who struggle to hear might have gaps in their education, and display social and behavioural difficulties.	National Deaf Children's Society: https://www.ndcs.org.uk/information-and-support/childhood-deafness/causes-of-deafness/glue-ear/ NHS: https://www.nhs.uk/conditions/glue-ear/
Syndrome Without A Name (SWAN)	Children with physical and/or learning difficulties that are not yet identified or understood are described as having SWAN. SEND provision will vary significantly depending upon the nature of the child's difficulties.	SWAN UK: https://www.undiagnosed.org.uk/

Legislation, policies and procedures

This chapter will help you to understand the legislation that is the foundation for all special educational needs and disabilities practice. By understanding the legislation which sets out the rights and legal entitlements of children with special educational needs and disability (SEND) and their families, and the statutory government guidance which is founded in legislation, you will be able to:

1. Understand your personal, legal responsibilities as an early years' practitioner, so you can deliver the best possible provision for the children in your care.

2. Understand the responsibilities of the proprietor of your setting, the local authority and central government, so you know exactly what help a child is entitled to by law.

3. Help other staff working with the child to know their duties.

4. Work in partnership with parents (this term covers anybody who has parental responsibility for a child) by raising their awareness of the child's and the whole family's legal entitlements, signposting them towards government guidance and sources of support. Remember, a child's wellbeing depends upon the strength of their family.

5. Write, or contribute towards writing, more effective Education, Health and Care Plans (EHCPs). EHCPs were brought about by the Children and Families Act 2014 and the Special Educational Needs and Disability Regulations 2014. By familiarising yourself with this legislation and the SEND Code, you put yourself in a stronger position to contribute towards EHCPs that will be approved by the local authority. This means that the child will receive the help that they require more swiftly and the process runs more smoothly than it otherwise might have done.

Later in the chapter we relate legislation and government guidance to your setting's policies and procedures. The law is the foundation of your setting's SEND policy, so we talk about what details your policy needs to cover in order to comply with the law, to reassure parents, and to demonstrate to Ofsted that you fully understand your legal responsibilities and the steps that you follow in order to carry out your duties. A thorough SEND policy helps to ensure that all children are at the heart of high-quality, inclusive practice and receive the consistent early years' provision they need in order to thrive. We also touch upon other policies that need to be written and reviewed with particular children's special educational needs and disabilities in mind.

We have done our best to break down legislation into manageable need-to-know parts, and we have eliminated legal jargon as far as possible. If you need further details you can always read the original legislation – links are provided in 'References' section on page 117. When you progress through this book you will probably find that you refer back to this chapter, dipping in and out as appropriate.

Ultimately, the aim of this chapter is to improve the lives of children with SEND.

Legislation

We've set out legislation in chronological order so you can see how one Act laid the foundation for another. All the legislation here is still in force today and so it's important for you to have a general understanding of it. The legislation that needs the closest study because it's the most relevant to you is Children and Families Act 2014, the Special Educational Needs and Disability Regulations 2014 and the Equality Act 2010. For maintained nursery schools all three pieces of legislation are imperative, and for private nurseries and childminders the Equality Act 2010 is the most significant.

The Children Act 1989

The Children Act 1989 covers *'provision of services for children in need, their families and others'*.

Under this Act, children in need are defined as those, *'unlikely to achieve or maintain, or to have the opportunity of achieving or maintaining, a reasonable standard of **health** or **development** without the provision of services by a local authority...or he is **disabled**.'*

Health is defined as physical or mental health.

Development covers behavioural, emotional, intellectual, physical and social development.

The Act makes it clear that local authorities must provide a range of services for the welfare of children in need. This means that local authorities must also support families so that they are in a position to provide high quality care for their children.

In order to make a decision about what services to provide a particular child local authorities must, where possible:

(a) *ascertain the child's wishes and feelings regarding the provision of those services; and*

(b) *give due consideration (having regard to his age and understanding) to such wishes and feelings of the child as they have been able to ascertain.*
Section 17, 4 (A)

The services local authorities provide *'may include providing accommodation, giving assistance in kind or cash'* - Section 17 (6)

Any assistance can be provided unconditionally or conditionally. In other words, local authorities can impose conditions, such as asking parents to pay some or all of the money back in future. However, when imposing conditions local authorities must have *'**regard to the means of the child concerned and each of his parents**'* - Section 17 (8)

Parents are not liable to make any repayment of assistance when they are in receipt of income support, of any element of child tax credit other than the family element, working tax credit, jobseeker's allowance or any income or employment and support allowance. Normally, parents are not liable to make repayments when in receipt of Universal Credit but there are exceptions.

Chapter 2: Legislation, policies and procedures

The UN Convention on the Rights of the Child (UNCRC)

The UN Convention on the Rights of the Child (UNCRC) applies to all children under the age of 18. It was adopted by the UN General Assembly in 1989 and agreed by the UK in 1991. The UNCRC is the foundation for all children's legislation written after 1991.

Here is a short summary of children's rights:
- All decisions and actions that affect children must prioritise children's best interests.
- Every child has a right to:
  - A standard of living that meets their emotional, intellectual, physical and social needs.
  - Express their opinions on decisions and actions that affect them, and to have their views taken seriously.
  - Join organisations and groups in order to meet other children, as long as it does not adversely affect the rights of others.
- Children with disabilities have the right to:
  - Live a fulfilling life, and to be independent as far as possible.
  - Be actively involved in the community.

The UNCRC has 54 articles covering all aspects of children's rights. Articles 2, 3, 12, 18, 23, 29 and 31 are particularly relevant to children with SEND, and can be found here: https://www.unicef.org.uk/what-we-do/un-convention-child-rights/

The United Nations Convention on the Rights of People with Disabilities (CRPD)

The UK ratified the United Nations Convention on the Rights of People with Disabilities (UNCRPD) in 2009. Below is a summary of some Articles included in the UNCRPD.

Article 3 sets out the general principles of the Convention:

(a) *Respect for inherent dignity, individual autonomy including the freedom to make one's own choices, and independence of persons;*

(b) *Non-discrimination;*

(c) *Full and effective participation and inclusion in society;*

(d) *Respect for difference and acceptance of persons with disabilities as part of human diversity and humanity;*

(e) *Equality of opportunity;*

(f) *Accessibility;*

(g) *Equality between men and women;*

(h) *Respect for the evolving capacities of children with disabilities and respect for the right of children with disabilities to preserve their identities.*

Article 7 (Children with disabilities), states that all actions concerning a child with disabilities must have the best interests of the child as a '*primary consideration*'. A child with disabilities must enjoy all human rights and freedoms '*on an equal basis with other children*'. The child also has '*the right to express their views freely on all matters affecting them, their views being given due weight in accordance with their age and maturity, on an equal basis with other children, and be provided with disability and age-appropriate assistance to realize that right*'.

Article 24 (Education), is about ensuring an inclusive education system at all levels with learning directed to:

(a) *The full development of human potential and sense of dignity and self-worth, and the strengthening of respect for human rights, fundamental freedoms and human diversity;*

(b) *The development by persons with disabilities of their personality, talents and creativity, as well as their mental and physical abilities, to their fullest potential;*

(c) *Enabling persons with disabilities to participate effectively in a free society;*
Clause 1

Both United Nation's conventions (the UNCRC and the CRPD) are reflected in UK legislation, particularly the Equality Act 2010 and the Children and Families Act 2014.

The Children and Families Act 2014 – Part 3

Part 3 of the Children and Families Act 2014 is about children and young people in England with special educational needs and disability (SEND). The Children and Families Act 2014 improved upon The Children Act 1989 by giving families better control over the welfare of their children. The aim of the 2014 Act is to ensure that high quality support is received by children with SEND and their families.

The Children and Families Act 2014 should be studied alongside the Special Educational Needs and Disability Regulations 2014 (see below). The function of the Regulations is to put into practice the powers granted by the Act by providing more detailed explanations.

As a result of the Act:

- Services for children with SEND are planned and run jointly between education, health care, social care services and local authorities.
- We now have Education Health and Care Plans (EHCPs) which are based on a single assessment. These plans support people from 0-25 years old and their families (see Chapter 5).

- Parents can have a personal budget which they can access to support their children's education, health and social care needs, if they choose.
- Local authorities are required to make sure families of children with SEND are clearly informed about all the services and provisions that are available to them locally. This is called the 'local offer' (discussed below).
- Parents and children, where practical, are involved in decisions relating to their own lives, and the local authority must provide them with all the information that they need to participate fully in those decisions. Families must also be provided with impartial advice, support and mediation services.

How are 'special educational needs and disabilities' defined under the Act?

A child is only considered to have special educational needs '*if he or she has a learning difficulty or disability which calls for special educational provision to be made for him or her*'.

A child under compulsory school age has a learning difficulty or disability '*if he or she is likely to be within subsection (2) when of compulsory school age (or would be likely, if no special educational provision were made)*'.

Subsection (2) – which is under Section 20 - states that a learning difficulty or disability is present if a child:

(a) *has a significantly greater difficulty in learning than the majority of others of the same age, or*

(b) *has a disability which prevents or hinders him or her from making use of facilities of a kind generally provided for others of the same age in mainstream schools or mainstream post-16 institutions.*

Subsection (4) makes it clear that a learning difficulty or disability is **not** '*solely because the language (or form of language) in which he or she is or will be taught is different from a language (or form of language) which is or has been spoken at home*'.

What is 'special educational provision'?
Section 21, subsection (1) defines special educational provision, health care provision and social care provision as '*provision that is additional to or different from that which*

would normally be provided for children or young people of the same age in a mainstream education setting'.

For a child under two, special educational provision *'means educational provision of any kind'*. For a child aged two or more it means *'educational or training provision that is additional to, or different from, that made generally for others of the same age...'*

Section 21, subsections (3), (4) and (5) define health care provision and social care provision:

'Health care provision' means the provision of health care services as part of the comprehensive health service in England continued under section 1(1) of the National Health Service Act 2006.[5]

'Social care provision' means the provision made by a local authority in the exercise of its social services functions.

Health care provision or social care provision which educates or trains a child or young person is to be treated as special educational provision (instead of health care provision or social care provision).

Local authority - identifying children with special educational needs and disabilities (SEND)

Under the Act, local authorities have a duty to identify all children in their area who **may have** SEND. This means they need to put systems in place to gather information from other services including educational institutions.

...the local authority in England must exercise its functions with a view to securing that it identifies—

(a) all the children and young people in its area who have or may have special educational needs, and

(b) all the children and young people in its area who have a disability.
Section 22

Local authorities have a duty to identify all children in their area who **have** or **may have** special needs and disabilities.

However, where a child is under compulsory school age it is the job **of health bodies to bring children who they believe have special educational needs to the attention of the local authority** – this is covered under Section 23 of the Act. Health bodies (clinical commissioning groups, NHS trusts or NHS foundations) must bring the child to the attention of the local authority after they:

(a) inform the child's parent of their opinion...

(b) give the child's parent an opportunity to discuss their opinion with an officer of the group or trust.

It is the responsibility of the health body to inform the parent of the existence of any voluntary organisation that they believe will be able to *'give the parent advice or assistance in connection with any special educational needs or disability the child may have'.*

Local authorities are responsible for children with SEND

Local authorities are responsible for all children in their area who have SEND.

A local authority in England is responsible for a child or young person if he or she is in the authority's area and has been—

(a) identified by the authority as someone who has or may have special educational needs, or

(b) brought to the authority's attention by any person as someone who has or may have special educational needs.

Section 24

Promoting integration and joint commissioning arrangements

Sections 25 and 26 place a duty on local authorities to promote integration between educational establishments, health care provision and social care provision for the benefit of children with SEND and their families. The purpose of these joint commissioning arrangements is so that education, health and care arrangements can be jointly planned.

Together, these bodies must agree:

- The education, health and social care provision needed by children with SEND, how this provision will be secured and by whom.
- How complaints about education, health and social care provision will be acted upon.
- How education, health and social care assessments should be secured.

Keep service under review

Section 27 states that local authorities are duty-bound to keep their SEND provision under review to ensure it continues to meet the educational and social care needs of the children concerned. In order to do this, local authorities must consult the following people in their area:

- Children with SEND and their parents.
- The governing bodies of maintained schools and nursery schools.
- The providers of early years education.

The local offer

Section 30 of the Act refers to the local authority's 'local offer'. Every local authority publishes their local offer on their website. The local offer is designed to be the go-to place where families who have children with SEND, can find the education, health and social care provision that the local authority expects to be available to them in the local area.

'A local authority in England must publish information about...the provision...it expects to be available in its area at the time of publication for children... who have special educational needs or a disability...'

The local authority's 'local offer' website has two clear purposes which are set out in the SEND code of practice, paragraph 4.2:

- *'To provide clear, comprehensive, accessible and up-to-date information about the available provision and how to access it, and*
- *To make provision more responsive to local needs and aspirations by directly involving disabled children and those with SEN and their parents, and disabled young people and those with SEN, and service providers in its development and review.'*

The SEND code of practice, paragraph 4.30 states:

'The local offer must include information about:
- *special educational, health and social care provision for children and young people with SEN or disabilities...*
- *details of how parents and young people can request an assessment for an EHC plan*
- *arrangements for identifying and assessing children and young people's SEN – this should include arrangements for EHC needs assessments*
- *other educational provision, for example sports or arts provision...*
- *arrangements for travel to and from schools, post-16 institutions and early years providers*
- *support to help children and young people move between phases of education (for example from early years to school, from primary to secondary)*
- *sources of information, advice and support in the local authority's area relating to SEN and disabilities including information and advice provided under Section 32 of the Children and Families Act 2014, forums for parents and carers and support groups*
- *childcare, including suitable provision for disabled children and those with SEN*
- *leisure activities*
- *arrangements for resolving disagreements and for mediation, and details about making complaints*
- *parents' and young people's rights to appeal a decision of the local authority to the First-tier*

Tribunal (SEN and disability) in respect of SEN and provision
- *the local authority's accessibility strategy (under paragraph 1 Schedule 10 of the Equality Act 2010)*
- *institutions approved under Section 41 of the Children and Families Act 2014.'*

A local authority *'must keep its local offer under review and may from time to time revise it'*. Section 30(6) of the Children and Families Act 2014 is clear that a local authority must publish and respond constructively to comments about its local offer that it has received from parents, and must give details of any actions it intends to take as a result of those comments.

Early years settings *'must co-operate with each other in the development and review of the Local Offer. This is essential so that the Local Offer provides a comprehensive, transparent and accessible picture of the range of services available'* (Early Years: guide to the 0-25 SEND Code of Practice, p.7).

The local offer is also a tool for the local authority. It helps them to measure how well their services are meeting local need.

Education Health and Care Needs Assessment ('EHCNA' or 'EHC assessment')

Chapter 4 covers EHCNAs (or EHC assessments) in depth. An EHCNA is an assessment of the educational, health and social care needs of a child, and it may or may not lead to an Education, Health and Care Plan (EHCP) being put in place for the child.

Section 36(3) of the Act requires local authorities to consider carrying out an EHCNA when a request is made by a child's parent or by somebody else who is concerned that the child has a special educational need or disability (this could be the manager of an early years setting or even a family friend). Section 36(4) states that the local authority *'must consult the child's parent…when considering whether to carry out an EHC assessment'*. Subsection (7) requires the local authority to inform the parent that they have a right to *'express views to the authority'*, and *'submit evidence to the authority'*.

In order to decide whether or not to carry out an EHCNA the local authority will gather evidence from the child, their parent, and the relevant educational institution. The educational institution (the term 'educational institution' includes mainstream nursery schools) will have to show the local authority that the child has not made progress despite carrying out the 'graduated approach' (see Chapter 3 for more about the graduated approach). If the local authority is *'of the opinion that the child…has or may have special needs, and it may be necessary for special educational provision to be made for the child…in accordance with an EHCP'* then it must *'secure an EHC needs assessment'* – Section 36(8)

Section 36(9) states that once an EHCNA has been carried out, the local authority must notify the child's parent of:

'(a) the outcome of the assessment,

(b) whether it proposes to secure that an EHC plan is prepared for the child…, and

(c) the reasons for that decision.'

Education Health and Care Plan (EHCP)

In Chapter 5 we talk about EHCPs in detail. EHCPs came about as a direct result of the Children and Families Act 2014. Here, we look at how the Act sets out the duty of the local authority and educational institutions (including mainstream nursery schools) towards children with an EHCP. You may want to refer back to this section after reading Chapter 5.

Section 37 makes it clear that once a local authority has decided that an EHCP is needed for a child, then it is responsible for making sure the plan is prepared. Thereafter, it is responsible for maintaining that plan.

The right to mainstream education

Section 33 (2) states that local authorities must ensure that the EHCP provides for the child to be educated in a mainstream setting unless it is incompatible with:

'(a) the wishes of the child's parent or the young person, or

(b) the provision of efficient education for others.'

However, Section 33 (3) makes it clear that it is difficult for a maintained school or nursery school to exclude a child on grounds of 'incompatibility' since it must show *'that there are no reasonable steps that it could take to prevent the incompatibility'*.

The purposes of an EHCP

The purposes of an EHCP are set out in Section 37(2). The plan must specify:

'(a) the child's…special educational needs;

(b) the outcomes sought for him or her;

(c) the special educational provision required by him or her;

(d) any health care provision reasonably required by the learning difficulties and disabilities which result in him or her having special educational needs;

(f) any social care provision reasonably required by the learning difficulties and disabilities…'

Education, Health and Care Plan (EHCP) - draft

Section 38(1) specifies that when a local authority is required to secure an EHCP for a child it *'must consult the child's parent…about the content of the plan during the preparation of the draft…'*

Section 38 states that the local authority must send the draft plan to the child's parent. This draft plan *'must not name a school or other institution, or specify a type of school or other institution'*.

At the same time that the local authority sends the draft plan to the parent it must inform the parent of their right to give feedback on the draft plan and the time limit for doing so. At this point the parent can request that the local authority secures a place for their child at a particular maintained school or nursery school.

Final Education, Health and Care Plan (EHCP)

Once a parent has requested that the local authority secure a place for their child at a particular educational institution, the local authority must then consult the *'governing body, proprietor or principal'* of that institution, or if the institution is in another local authority then that local authority must be contacted (Section 39).

In the final plan the requested educational institution is named, unless:

'(a) the school or other institution requested is unsuitable for the age, ability, aptitude or special educational needs of the child or young person concerned, or

(b) the attendance of the child or young person at the requested school or other institution would be incompatible with—

(i) the provision of efficient education for others, or

(ii) the efficient use of resources.'
Section 39(4)

If Section 39(4) applies, then the local authority must name an institution or a type of institution that they deem appropriate for the child - Section 39(5).

Under Section 39(8) the local authority must send a finalised copy of the EHCP to:

'(a) the child's parent…, and

(b) the governing body, proprietor or principal of any school or other institution named in the plan.'

Institutions with a duty to admit a child with an EHCP

Under Section 43(2) *'the governing body, proprietor or principal of the school or other institution must admit the child or young person for whom the (EHC) plan is maintained'*.

Section 43(1) lists the institutions to which Section 43(2) applies, including:

'(a) a maintained school;

(b) a maintained nursery school;

(e) a non-maintained special school;

(f) an institution approved by the Secretary of State under section 41.'

Section 41 refers to independent special schools and nurseries.

EHCP reviews and reassessments

Section 44(1) sets out the timeline for local authorities to review EHCPs:

'(a) in the period of 12 months starting with the date on which the plan was first made, and

(b) in each subsequent period of 12 months starting with the date on which the plan was last reviewed under this section.'

Under Section 44(2) the local authority must secure a reassessment of an EHCP if the child's parent or the governing body, proprietor or principal of the setting request it. A local authority can also decide to carry out a reassessment at any other time it thinks necessary.

During a review or reassessment a local authority must consult with the child's parent – Section 44(6).

Once an EHCP has been secured, the local authority has a responsibility to maintain the plan. The EHCP plan must be kept *'under review'* to ensure that it continually meets the child's educational, health and social needs.

Ceasing to maintain an EHCP

Section 45 sets out the circumstances under which a local authority may cease to maintain an EHCP. These circumstances are when the local authority is no longer responsible for the child, or believes the child no longer requires the special educational provision specified in the plan.

However, parents have the right to appeal against this decision and the local authority *'may not cease to maintain an EHC plan for a child...until after the end of the period allowed for bringing an appeal against its decision, or when the appeal has been finally determined...'*

Personal budgets and direct payments

A local authority that maintains an EHCP must prepare a personal budget for the child if requested to do so by the child's parent during the draft EHCP stage – this is detailed in Section 49 (1). When preparing a personal budget, the local authority identifies an amount it will make available so that the child can access all the provisions and resources specified in the EHCP.

'The authority prepares a "personal budget" for the child or young person if it identifies an amount as available to secure particular provision that is specified, or proposed

to be specified, in the EHC plan, with a view to the child's parent or the young person being involved in securing the provision.'
Section 49(2)

Parents can arrange for the local authority to make direct payments into their personal bank account. This enables them to buy and manage services themselves. Alternatively, they could ask the setting to hold the money for them (in this case the setting will need to ask their permission before money is spent). Parents can decide whether to spend the budget on education needs, transport requirements, social care or health. However, the money must be used to secure the provision documented in the EHCP. The idea of a personal budget is to provide parents with greater control and choice over the support their child receives.

The Children and Families Act 2014 makes reference to The Special Educational Needs (Personal Budgets) Regulations 2014 – the link is provided under 'References' on page 117. Under these Regulations you will find details about:

- Who can receive direct payments and under what conditions.
- How the local authority decides whether or not to make direct payments.
- Conditions for direct payments.
- How the use of direct payments by the recipient is monitored and reviewed by the local authority.

Appealing local authority's decisions

If a child's parent disagrees with the local authority's decision relating to the EHCNA or EHCP process they have the right to appeal to the First-tier Tribunal subject to mediation.

Under Section 51(2) reasons for appealing are:

- That the local authority has decided not to secure an EHCNA for the child.
- Following an EHCNA the local authority has decided that an EHCP is unnecessary.
- The parent doesn't believe that the special educational provision specified in the plan meets the child's needs.
- The parent thinks the educational institution named in the plan isn't right for the child.
- No educational institution is named in the final plan.
- The local authority has received a request to reassess the

needs of the child but they have decided not to do so.
- The local authority has decided not to amend or replace an EHCP following a review or reassessment.
- The local authority has decided to cease maintaining an EHCP.

Under Section 51(3) a child's parent can appeal to the First-tier Tribunal:

'(a) when an EHC plan is first finalised for the child or young person, and

(b) following an amendment or replacement of the plan.'

Right to mediation

Before making certain appeals parents are required to attend mediation with the local authority. Mediation is a chance for parents to sit down informally with the local authority to try to reach a solution together. This is a way of avoiding the stress and cost of a formal appeals process.

Section 52(2) specifies that the local authority must inform parents of their right to mediation following any big decisions, including when an EHCP is made, amended or replaced.

If a parent decides to pursue mediation then they must inform the local authority of this and the issues they wish to discuss - Section 52(3).

The SEND Code of Practice 0-25, paragraphs 11.42 and 11.43, summarise the role and function of the appeals process:

'The Tribunal hears appeals against decisions made by the local authorities in England in relation to children's and young people's EHC needs assessments and EHC plans. It also hears disability discrimination claims against schools and against local authorities when the local authority is the responsible body for a school.'

'The Tribunal seeks to ensure that the process of appealing is as user friendly as possible, and to avoid hearings that are overly legalistic or technical. It is the Tribunal's aim to ensure that a parent or young person should not need to engage legal representation when appealing a decision. Parents and young people may find it helpful to have support from a voluntary organisation or friend at a hearing'.

information about how they provide equal opportunities for disabled children.

"SEN information" is—

(i) *the arrangements for the admission of disabled persons as pupils at the school;*

(ii) *the steps taken to prevent disabled pupils from being treated less favourably than other pupils;*

(iii) *the facilities provided to assist access to the school by disabled pupils.'*

Under this section a 'disabled person' is defined as under the Equality Act 2010 (see page 40).

Section 35 (2) states that: *'those concerned with making special educational provision for the child must secure that the child engages in the activities of the school together with children who do not have special educational needs…'* However, this only applies *'as far as is reasonably practicable'* with:

'(a) the child receiving the special educational provision called for by his or her special educational needs,

(b) *the provision of efficient education for the children with whom he or she will be educated, and*

(c) *the efficient use of resources.'*

Supply of goods and services

Section 64 gives a local authority powers to supply goods and services to maintained schools and nursery schools that are attended (or likely to be attended) by a child with an EHCP. These 'goods and services' could be in the form of equipment or specialist services to support the child. For example, a child with a sensory impairment may need to be supported by a Qualified Teacher for Children with Vision Impairment.

Using 'best endeavours' to secure special educational provision

Section 66 requires that governing bodies, proprietors and management committees of maintained schools and nursery schools *'use its best endeavours to secure that the special educational provision called for by the pupil's or student's special educational needs is made'*.

The phrase 'best endeavours' means that they must do everything possible to fulfil their legal duties.

Equal opportunities

Section 69 states that the governing bodies of maintained schools and maintained nurseries must prepare a SEN Information Report containing

Special Educational Needs and Disability Regulations 2014

The Regulations stem from the Children and Families Act 2014. It is helpful to understand the following Regulations in order to contribute to effective EHCPs (see Chapter 5).

Regulation 6 (1)

Once the Education and Health Care Needs Assessment (EHCNA) has started the local authority must gather information and advice about the needs of the child and what provision is needed to meet those needs. The local authority must gather this information from:

- The child's parent.
- The head of the educational setting or another person responsible for the child's education.
- Health care professionals identified by the responsible commissioning body.
- An educational psychologist.
- Social care.
- Any other person the local authority thinks is appropriate.

Regulation 6 (4)

If the advice in Regulation 6 (1) has already been provided to the local authority, the local authority cannot request the advice a second time. The only exception is when the child's parents, the local authority or the person who provided that advice does not think the existing advice is sufficient for an EHC needs assessment.

Regulation 8 (1)

Every organisation or person who has been contacted by the local authority for information and advice in regard to the EHC needs assessment *must comply with such a request within 6 weeks of the date on which they receive it*. The organisation or person does not have to comply with the time limit in exceptional circumstances such as if the child is absent for a continuous period of 4 weeks or more during that 6-week period, or if the child fails to keep an appointment in that 6-week period.

Regulation 10 (1)

Following an EHC needs assessment the local authority must (under the Children and Families Act, Section 36) inform the child's parents of the outcome of the assessment, whether or not it will secure an EHCP and the reasons for their decision. Regulation 10 (1) says that if the local authority has decided against the EHCP then they must notify the child's parents *'as soon as practicable, and in any event within 16 weeks of the local authority receiving a request for an EHC needs assessment'*.

Regulation 12

In the EHCP the local authority must communicate:

- The views, interests and aspirations of the child and their parents.
- The child's special educational needs.
- The child's health care needs which relate to their special educational needs (this must be agreed by the clinical commissioning group responsible for the child's care).
- The child's social care needs which relate to their special educational needs or disability.
- The special educational provision required by the child and the outcomes sought as a result of this provision.
- Any health or social care provision reasonably required which result in the child having special educational needs.
- Any social care provision which must be made for the child under Section 2 of the Chronically Sick and Disabled Persons Act 1970 (this Act is available online).
- The type of institution the child will attend (eg. maintained nursery school) and, if known, the name of the institution.
- If the special educational provision is going to be paid for by direct payment then the EHCP must state the outcomes to be met by the direct payment. For more about direct payments see 'Personal budgets' under the Children and Families Act 2014.
- The advice and information obtained in accordance with Regulation 6 (1) must be set out in the appendices.

Regulation 13 (1)

When the local authority sends the draft EHCP to the child's parent it must advise them where they can find details of institutions their child could attend. The local authority must give the parent at least 15 days (beginning with the day the draft plan was served) in which to:

- Feedback their opinions about the content of the draft plan.
- Request that a particular institution be named in the plan.
- Arrange a meeting with the local authority to discuss the draft plan.

Regulation 13 (2)

The local authority must send the final EHCP to:

- The child's parent.
- The governing body, principal or proprietor of the institution named in the EHC plan.
- The responsible commissioning body (the relevant health and social care professional involved in the EHCP).

The local authority must send the plan 'as soon as is practicable, and in any event within 20 weeks of the local authority receiving a request for an EHC needs assessment'.

Regulation 19

'When undertaking a review of an EHC plan, a local authority must—

'(a) consult the child and the child's parent or the young person, and take account of their views, wishes and feelings;

(b) consider the child or young person's progress towards achieving the outcomes specified in the EHC plan and whether these outcomes remain appropriate for the child or young person;

(c) consult the school or other institution attended by the child or young person.'

Regulation 20

Paragraph (1)

Reviews of the child's EHCP must take place at the educational institution the child attends.

Paragraph (2)

The following persons must be invited to attend the review meeting:

- The child's parent.
- The child's education provider (headteacher, principal, proprietor or manager).
- A special educational needs education officer from the local authority.
- A special educational needs social services officer from the local authority.
- Health care professionals identified by the responsible commissioning body to provide care for the child.

Paragraph (3)

At least two weeks' notice of the date of the review meeting must be given to those invited.

Paragraph (4)

'The person arranging the review meeting must obtain advice and information about the child or young person from the persons referred to in paragraph (2) and must circulate it to those persons at least two weeks in advance of the review meeting.'

Paragraph (5)

'The child or young person's progress towards achieving the outcomes specified in the EHC plan must be considered at the meeting.'

Paragraph (7)

Where a child attends a school ('school' includes maintained nursery schools), the local authority must ask the head teacher or principal to write a report on the child, setting out their recommendations on any amendments to the EHCP following the meeting. The head teacher or principal must highlight the differences between their recommendations and those of others who attended the meeting.

Paragraph (8)

Where a child does not attend a school, the local authority must prepare a written report on the child 'setting out its recommendations on any amendments to be made to the EHC plan, and referring to any difference between those recommendations and recommendations of others attending the meeting'.

Paragraph (9)
'*The written report must include advice and information about the child or young person obtained in accordance with paragraph (4) and must be prepared within two weeks of the review meeting, and sent to everyone referred to in paragraph (2).*'

Paragraph (10)
The local authority must then decide whether it will continue to maintain the EHCP as it is, amend it, or stop maintaining it altogether. It must notify the child's parent and the people referred to in paragraph (2) within 4 weeks of the review meeting.

Paragraph (11)
If the local authority wants to stop maintaining the EHCP it must notify the child's parents of their right to appeal the decision under Section 51 (2) (e) of the Children and Families Act 2014. The local authority must inform parents of:

- The time limits for appealing.
- Information concerning mediation (Children's and Families Act 2014, Section 52).
- The availability of disagreement resolution services.
- The availability of information and advice regarding children's special educational needs.

Regulation 21

Paragraph (1)
This Regulation applies when a child does not attend a school or other institution and so the local authority is responsible for carrying out the EHCP review.

Paragraph (2)
The following persons must be invited to attend the review meeting:

- The child's parent.
- A special educational needs education officer from the local authority.
- A special educational needs social services officer from the local authority.
- Health care professionals identified by the responsible commissioning body to provide care for the child.
- Any other person the local authority deems appropriate.

Paragraph (3)
At least two weeks' notice of the date of the review meeting must be given to those invited.

Paragraph (4)
'*The local authority must obtain advice and information about the child or young person from the persons referred to in paragraph (2) and must circulate it to those persons at least two weeks in advance of the review meeting.*'

Paragraph (5)
'*The meeting must consider the child or young person's progress towards achieving the outcomes specified in the EHC plan.*'

Paragraph (7)
'*The local authority must prepare a report on the child or young person within two weeks of the review meeting setting out its recommendations on any amendments required to be made to the EHC plan, and should refer to any difference between those recommendations and recommendations of others attending the meeting.*'

Paragraph (8)
'*The written report must include advice and information about the child or young person obtained in accordance with paragraph (4) and must be prepared within two weeks of the review meeting, and sent to everyone referred to in paragraph (2).*'

Paragraph (9)
The local authority must then decide whether it will continue to maintain the EHCP as it is, amend it, or stop maintaining it altogether. It must notify the child's parent within 4 weeks of the review meeting.

Paragraph (10)
If the local authority wants to stop maintaining the EHCP it must notify the child's parent of their right to appeal the decision under Section 51 of the Children and Families Act 2014. The local authority must inform the parent of:

- The time limits for appealing.
- Information concerning mediation (Children's and Families Act 2014, Section 52).
- The availability of disagreement resolution services
- The availability of information and advice regarding children's special educational needs.

Chapter 2: Legislation, policies and procedures

Regulation 22

Paragraph (1)

This Regulation covers what happens when a local authority decides to amend an existing EHCP.

Paragraph (2)

Following a review, if a local authority is considering amending an EHCP it must advise the child's parent where they can find information about educational institutions for their child, and it must:

- Send the child's parent a copy of the EHCP specifying the amendments, together with copies of evidence to support the amendments.
- Inform the child's parent that they can request that the local authority secure a place at the educational institution named in the EHCP for their child.
- Give the parent 15 days' notice (beginning with the day on which the draft plan was served) to:
  - Make comments on the draft EHCP or to arrange a meeting with an officer of the local authority to talk through their comments instead of submitting them in writing.
  - Request that a particular educational institution be named on the plan.

Paragraph (3)

The local authority must send the amended EHCP to the child's parent, the educational institution named on the EHCP, and to the responsible commissioning body. The local authority must send the plan '*as soon as practicable, and in any event within 8 weeks of the local authority sending a copy of the EHC plan…*'

Paragraph (4)

If the local authority decides not to amend the EHCP it must notify the child's parent of its decision and reasons for its decision '*as soon as practicable and in any event within 8 weeks of the local authority sending a copy of the EHC plan…*'

Paragraph (5)

If the local authority wants to stop maintaining the EHCP it must notify the child's parent of their right to appeal the decision under Section 51 of the Children and Families Act 2014. The local authority must inform the parent of:

- The time limits for appealing.

- Information concerning mediation (Children's and Families Act 2014, Section 52).
- The availability of disagreement resolution services (mediation).
- The availability of information and advice regarding children's special educational needs.

The Equality Act 2010

The Equality Act 2010 defines a disabled person as someone who has a mental or physical impairment which has a long-term, substantial effect on their ability to carry out daily tasks.

Early years settings in schools are covered in Part 6 of the Equality Act 2010. Early years settings must not discriminate against a child by not offering the child a place in the setting, or by only offering a place under specific terms and conditions. They must ensure that the child has full access to education, facilities and services. They must not subject '*the pupil to any (other) detriment*' which means they must not subject a child to any form of disadvantage. The Equality Act 2010 defines disability discrimination as:

- Penalising a child by failing to accommodate their needs. For example, by not allowing a guide dog in the setting or by penalising the child for having time off for medical appointments.
- Direct discrimination. When a child receives less favourable treatment than other children because of their disability.
- Indirect discrimination. This is '*…applying a provision, criterion or practice that puts, or would put, a disabled child at a disadvantage compared with another child who is not disabled. A blanket policy is a policy that is applied in the same way to all children. A blanket policy may put a disabled child at a particular disadvantage.*' When a setting has a policy or particular method of working that has a negative impact on a disabled child then a watertight justification must be provided.
- Failure to make 'reasonable adjustments' to accommodate disabled children. See further below for more about reasonable adjustments.
- Harassment is prohibited under the Equality Act 2010. '*Harassment is behaviour which violates the dignity of a disabled child, or crates an intimidating, hostile,*

degrading, humiliating or offensive environment for them. Harassment would include bullying, mocking or belittling a disabled child'.

- Victimisation. When a child is poorly treated because their parents have made a complaint against the setting.

For details about what constitutes disability discrimination under the Equality Act 2010 visit the Equality and Human Rights Commission's website: https://www.equalityhumanrights.com/en/publication-download/reasonable-adjustments-disabled-pupils

Early years settings that are not based in schools are termed 'service providers' in the Equality Act 2010 and they must comply with Part 3 of the Act. Part 3 states that service providers '*must not discriminate against a person requiring the service by not providing the person with the service*'. Service providers must also not terminate a service as a result of disability and must not subject the disabled child to '*any other detriment*'.

Disability discrimination claims can be brought against early years settings, schools and local authorities. If a claim is successful the institution could be ordered to:

- Admit the child if the child has been turned away.
- Arrange staff training.
- Change guidance or policies.
- Write a written apology.
- Make up for activities or other opportunities the child has missed.
- Make 'reasonable adjustments' – see below.

An institution will never be ordered to give financial compensation, make physical alterations to the building, or to dismiss a member of staff.

A disability discrimination claim should be a last resort. The parent's first step should be a formal, written complaint to the institution. If this doesn't bring satisfactory results, the next step before taking legal action would be to complain to the Department for Education and Ofsted.

Reasonable adjustments

Under the Equality Act 2010, all early years settings and schools must make 'reasonable adjustments' to ensure that a disabled child is not discriminated against.[6] To make reasonable adjustments, providers must anticipate where disadvantage to a child may arise and make changes and adaptations in advance. Before a disabled child is due to start at a setting, the setting needs to plan ahead and anticipate any barriers that child might face in order to plan 'reasonable adjustments'. Reasonable adjustments could include reviewing policies, raising staff awareness, arranging training for staff so that they can meet the child's particular needs, providing resources to support the child, changing the arrangement of the room, or making adjustments to routines.

The reasonable adjustments duty includes three key requirements:

- To make adjustments to any provision, criterion or practice.
- To make alternations to physical features.
- To provide auxiliary aids and services.

Reasonable adjustments have to be made if it is reasonable for the setting to do so, taking into account:

- How much time the child spends at the school or setting.
- How effective the adjustments would be in helping the disabled child overcome disadvantage.
- The financial resources available.
- How the adjustments will affect health and safety.
- The interests of the other children.

Although the '*responsible body*' – whoever is in charge of the setting – is ultimately responsible for complying with the Equality Act 2010, the setting can be charged with unlawful discrimination if any member of staff has placed a disabled child at a disadvantage.

Under the Equality Act 2010 there can be '*justification*' for actions that would otherwise amount to discrimination against the child. Justifications could include excluding a disabled child for the safety of the other children in the setting. However, any justification must be proven to be legitimate and not as a result of the setting's failure to plan ahead for the disabled child or to make '*reasonable adjustments*'.

The Equality and Human Rights Commission have published 'Reasonable adjustments for disabled children'. Although the guidance is aimed at schools, it is also useful for early years settings: https://www.equalityhumanrights.com/en/publication-download/reasonable-adjustments-disabled-pupils

Coronavirus: keeping up-to-date with legislation

On 1st May 2020 temporary changes were made to the Children and Families Act 2014 regarding EHCPs and EHCNAs when the Coronavirus Act 2020 came into force. In May, June and July 2020, local authorities were expected to use 'reasonable endeavours' to secure or arrange EHCP provision rather than having a legally binding obligation.

'The duty on local authorities or health commissioning bodies to secure or arrange the provision is temporarily modified to a duty to use 'reasonable endeavours' to do so.'

The same applied to EHCNA and EHCP statutory timescales, as local authorities were given more flexibility:

'Where it is not reasonably practicable or impractical to meet that time limit for reason relating to the incidence of transmission of coronavirus (COVID-19), the specific time limit (such as to issue a plan to someone eligible for one within 20 weeks of the initial request) in the regulations being amended will not apply. Instead, the local authority or other body to whom that time limit applies will have to complete the process as soon as reasonably practicable…'
(Education, health and care needs assessments and plans: guidance on temporary legislative changes relating to coronavirus (COVID-19), updated 6th July 2020, Department for Education)

These temporary changes to the local authority's legally binding duty to secure or arrange EHCP provision ended at the start of the autumn term 2020, and the flexibility regarding timescales was only effective until 25 September 2020. However, government guidance is changing continually in response to the coronavirus pandemic and if local lockdowns occur there is a possibility that temporary measures will be introduced again, perhaps on a local level. To keep abreast of changes check the following websites:

https://www.ipsea.org.uk/news
(IPSEA: news)

https://councilfordisabledchildren.org.uk/news-opinion
(Council for Disabled Children: news)

If you have a Twitter account you could follow @AliceLIrving and @SteveBroach who are partners at Rook Irwin Sweeney LLP. They are specialists in education and SEND law and update their Twitter followers with the latest legal developments relating to coronavirus.

Note that at the time of writing a setting's legally binding duties towards children with SEND and their families under the Children and Families Act 2014 and the Equality Act 2010 remain unchanged. Early years settings cannot cite health and safety grounds as a reason not to admit a child with any special educational need or disability, unless agreement has been reached with a medical professional. Whatever the circumstances, settings must make 'reasonable adjustments' to ensure a child can attend and can access provision. If a setting is unable to do so they must be able to give compelling reasons for this.

Government guidance relating to the coronavirus can be found in Chapter 10: Resources and Training under the title 'Coronavirus guidance'.

Government guidance

This section summarises the government guidance linked to legislation. To gain a thorough understanding you will need to read the guidance in full – the website addresses are listed under 'References: Government guidance' on page 117.

SEND code of practice: 0-25 years

This guidance, which relates to the Children and Families Act 2014, informs SEND practice in England. (In Scotland the guidance is 'Additional support for learning: statutory guidance 2017', and the Welsh guidance is 'Special Educational Needs Code of Practice for Wales'.) The 'SEND code of practice: 0-25 years'– 'the Code' – clearly explains the duties of local authorities, health bodies, early years' providers, schools and colleges under the Act.

Every member of staff in schools and early years settings must understand how the Code affects their day-to-day role. The aim of the Code is to make sure that each child with SEND is seen as an individual so they develop, learn, participate and achieve in order to secure 'outcomes from education, health and social care which will make the biggest difference to their lives'.

The Code uses two key words **must** and **should**. The word 'must' indicates a statutory requirement, and 'should' indicates that something is not compulsory but is strongly recommended.

'(Early Years) *Providers* **must** *have arrangements in place to support children with SEN or disabilities. These arrangements* **should** *include a clear approach to identifying and responding to SEN. The benefits of early identification are widely recognised – identifying need at the earliest point, and then making effective provision, improves long-term outcomes for children.'* Paragraph 5.4

The Code states that EHCPs **should** *be clear, concise, understandable and accessible to parents, children, young people, providers and practitioners.'* Paragraph 9.61

See paragraphs 9.62 and 9.69 of the Code for specific details about what **must** be included in the EHCP. In brief, these details are:

- The child's goals and aspirations.
- The child's special educational needs.
- The child's health and social care needs related to their disability.
- The outcomes sought for the child (paragraphs 9.64 and 9.69 give guidance on outcomes).
- The special educational provision the child requires.
- Health and social care provision that 'educates or trains a child' (paragraph 9.73).
- The name and type of establishment the child will attend. The child's parents have a right to request a particular school for their child (paragraph 9.78).
- Details of how the personal budget will support the outcomes.
- Advice and information gathered during the EHC needs assessment must be attached.

Paragraphs 9.131 – 9.136 of the Code give information about the duties of local authorities to maintain EHCPs. Paragraphs 9.137 – 9.140 covers the duties of local authorities to maintain the social care provision in the EHCP, and paragraph 9.141 details the duties of health care services to maintain the health care provision in the EHCP.

Early years: guide to the 0-25 SEND code of practice

This guide is non-statutory and isn't a replacement for the SEND Code. It is simply designed to help early years providers to more fully understand their duties by drawing out elements of the Code that relate specifically to early years settings.

The guide covers:

- Duties of early years providers towards children with special educational needs and disabilities under the Children and Families Act 2014, the SEND Code of Practice 0-25, and the Equality Act 2010.
- Legal duties and responsibilities of the local authority towards children with SEND.
- Legal duties and responsibilities of early years providers:
  - To ensure that children with SEND receive an education that enables them to achieve the best possible educational outcomes.
  - To use their best endeavours to make sure that children with SEND receive the support they are entitled to and that they need.
  - Have high aspirations and expectations for **all children** in their setting.
- Importance of identifying children with SEND as early as possible.
- Importance of implementing SEN Support by working in partnership with parents and multidisciplinary support services including specialist teachers, health and social care specialists.
- Funding for SEN Support.
- Reviewing the progress of children with SEND using your everyday early years foundation stage (EYFS) formative assessments towards the Early Learning Goals.
- Progress check at age 2 and how this relates to children with SEND.

- Requesting an EHC needs assessment and the path to an EHC plan.
- Assessing and record keeping.
- The role of the SENCO and Area SENCO in early years provision.
- Local offer (see page 31). Early years settings must cooperate with local authorities to develop the local offer so that they can review the effectiveness of the services and provision that are available locally.

Ofsted's education inspection framework: 2019

In the previous Ofsted framework the effectiveness of SEND provision was focused on the progress made by children and the effective use of funding. The problem was that children's progress was very difficult to measure due to the range of special needs and difficulties included within this group. It was also impossible to compare progress between schools partly because they measured progress in different ways.

The Schools, Students and Teachers network (SSAT) senior education lead, Colin Logan, has explained that under the new Ofsted's framework, inspectors will not look

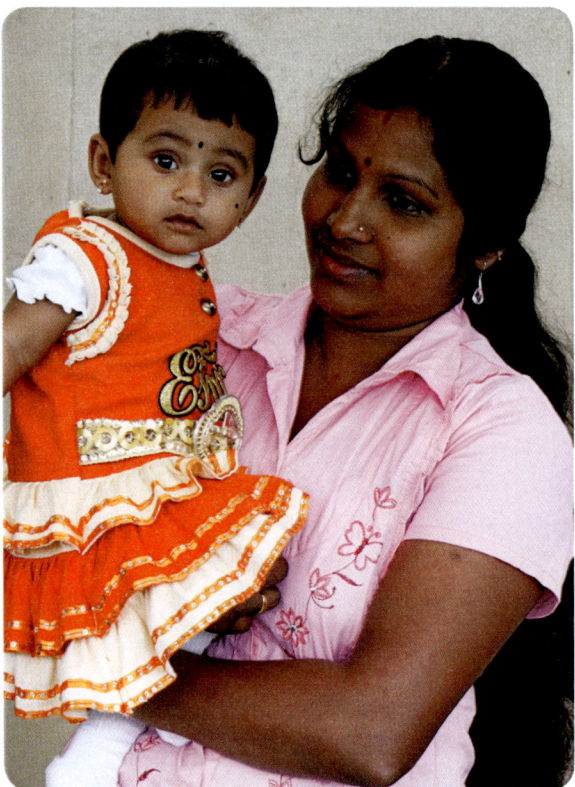

at progress data at all[7]. What they will be interested in is **what leaders have done as a result of the data they have collected**. How do assessments and data inform SEN support and the graduated approach? (see Chapter 3), and how does data raise children's achievement?

No longer will SEND provision be inspected as a separate category. This is because effective SEND provision should be integrated as seamlessly as possible into early years practice as a whole. Ofsted are looking to see that educational institutions provide inclusive, quality education for all. The new framework emphasises that **every section within the framework applies to children with SEND**.

Inspectors will judge '*whether leaders are ambitious for all pupils with SEND*' and how they '*develop and adapt the curriculum so that it is coherently sequenced to all pupils' needs, starting points and aspirations for the future*'. Educational settings will be judged on how well they include children with SEND so they can participate in the life of the setting as a whole. They will be judged upon whether outcomes for children with SEND are improving as a result of the provision made for them in terms of their:

- Communication and interaction
- Cognition and learning
- Physical and sensory needs
- Social and emotional health.

Inspectors will look at how **all children** are being prepared for the next stage of their lives by being given the best possible start in life – this is called 'cultural capital'. Cultural capital is about:

- Broadening minds by developing knowledge and understanding of people, communities and the wider world.
- Understanding children's different experiences and backgrounds.
- Inducing awe and wonder.
- Breaking down barriers to learning (see Chapter 7).

Inspectors will check to make sure that children with SEND are not being offered a reduced curriculum, but are able to acquire the knowledge and skills that they need to succeed in life. If, for example, a child is taken out of the setting for additional support with a specific skill does this mean that by leaving the room they are missing out on a curriculum experience that the other children are enjoying? If so, is there an alternative way that support could be provided?

The new framework raises the bar in terms of SEND. It is no longer just the responsibility of the SENCO and the setting manager, it is now **every member of staff's responsibility** to ensure that the needs of children with SEND are met. For a setting to receive an outstanding judgement children need to be achieving '*exceptionally well*', and to be judged as good children must have the '*best possible outcomes*'. A setting will be judged as inadequate if '*pupils with SEND do not benefit from a good quality education. Expectations of them are low, and their needs are not accurately identified, assessed or met*'.

SEND: guide for parents and carers

This is a guide you can signpost to parents and carers. It helps them to understand the SEND system and how it works to support the child and the whole family. It explains what schools, early years settings, the local authority, and health and social services must do to provide support. It explains to parents what they can do if they disagree with decisions made by various organisations.

'*The most important people in any child or young person's life are their parents. You know your children best of all. What you as parents think, feel and say is important. You should be listened to and you need to be fully involved in decisions that affect your children*.' Edward Timpson, Parliamentary Under Secretary of State for Children and Families, SEND: guide for parents and carers.

Short breaks

Families who have children with SEND, benefit from a break from their caring responsibilities and local authorities have a duty under the 'The Breaks for Carers of Disabled Children Regulations 2011'[8] to provide short break services and to make it clear how families can access these.

Breaks for children aim to provide parents with a break from caring, and also to enable the child to participate in interesting, stimulating activities.

There are two guides that practitioners can bring to parents' attention:

- 'Short breaks for disabled children'
- 'Short breaks for carers of disabled children'.

The websites for both guides are listed under 'References: Government guidance', see page 117.

Your setting's SEND policy and procedures

Having a clear SEND policy and set of procedures enables your setting to maintain a consistent, high quality level of provision for children and helps to keep everybody in the setting safe.

There is a difference between 'policy' and 'procedure'. A policy is a statement that says **how** you will work, and a procedure communicates the **actions you will take** in order to carry out the policy. In reality your SEND policy is both!

All policies and procedures are only effective if they are read, understood and followed by all staff and shared

Chapter 2: Legislation, policies and procedures

with parents too. Clear policies and procedures help to give staff the confidence of knowing what to do if a particular issue or set of circumstances occur.

Your setting's policies will be underpinned by current legislation and statutory government guidance. Here are some policies your setting might have in place that are relevant to children with SEND:

- Special Educational Needs and Disability (SEND)
- Inclusion
- Equal Opportunities
- Children's Rights.

Depending upon the size of your setting, some of these policies might be banded together. For example 'Inclusion' could incorporate SEND and Children's Rights. It is the function of your policy or policies to demonstrate that you understand your statutory duties to children under:

- Children and Families Act 2014
- Special Needs and Disability Regulations 2014
- Equality Act 2010
- SEND code of practice: 0-25
- Early Years Foundation Stage Statutory Framework (EYFS)

Special educational needs and disability (SEND) policy

Your SEND policy needs to address the following points in order to demonstrate that you understand your statutory duties towards children with SEND and the procedures you will follow to carry out these duties:

- All children have the right to a broad and balanced curriculum, whatever their background and needs.
- Your setting is open to everybody in the community and that families are made aware of your Equal Opportunities policy.
- Discriminatory behaviour and language is not tolerated and what your response will be if an incident occurs.
- How you work with parents, carers and outside agencies to ensure children's educational needs are met.
- It is your duty to identify special educational needs and disabilities and the procedures you follow once those needs are identified.
- You use your everyday EYFS formative assessments towards the Early Learning Goals (ELGs) and statutory progress checks to assess whether a child is developing at expected levels.
- Name the SENCO and what their role is, including how they assist in identifying special needs, plan strategies to address those needs, work with parents and other professionals, record and communicate children's progress, review SEND policies, and attend SEND training courses to ensure their knowledge is up-to-date and relevant.
- How and when you liaise with outside agencies and services such as speech and language therapists.
- At what stage you will request an EHCP.
- You provide additional resources and support when a child needs them to address a special educational need or disability.
- Resources reflect children's diversity so that they develop self-respect and respect for each other by avoiding stereotypes.
- How you provide an inclusive environment by adapting your teaching style and through your planning, approaches, and differentiated activities.
- Your physical environment is inclusive, eg. you have a disabled toilet, wheelchair ramps, wide-access doors.
- How you manage the transition of SEND children, eg. the move from preschool to school.

- How often you review your SEND policy, and your procedure for reviewing your policy, including requesting feedback from parents and staff about its effectiveness.
- Your complaints procedure in the event that parents are unhappy with your SEND provision.

Sharing your SEND policy with parents is part of your setting's statutory duty under the EYFS which states that early years providers:

'*…must provide information for parents on how they support children with SEN and disabilities, and should regularly review and evaluate the quality and breadth of the support they offer or can access for children with SEN or disabilities.*' (5.7)

Other policies related to SEND

The following policies are important for all children but may be particularly relevant to children in your setting who have specific emotional, health or social care needs:

- Administration of medicines
- Behaviour management plans
- Intimate care plans
- Manual handling
- Safeguarding and child protection.

When policies are written and reviewed they should be done so with the special educational needs and disabilities of the children in your setting in mind. In Chapter 8, for example, we focus on child protection and SEND because there are additional safeguarding measures to consider in order to keep vulnerable children safe. In fact, inclusion should be reflected across **all** of your setting's policies.

Personal Emergency Evacuation Plan (PEEP)

A Personal Emergency Evacuation Plan should be completed for any child who would need assistance in the event of an evacuation. The plan should consider whether:

- The child is in different rooms or buildings during the course of the day.
- The child can identify emergency exit signs and emergency exit routes.

- The child needs visuals to reduce their anxiety around a change of routine, such as a loud fire alarm noise.
- The child needs 1:1 support and who will provide that support if that member of staff is away.
- The child can hear emergency alarms, or see exits and exit routes.
- Steps, furniture or other obstacles may prevent the child's safe exit.
- The child is dependent on mobility equipment such as a wheelchair.

Some regional fire brigades publish PEEP templates on the internet. See Lancashire Fire and Rescue's template as an example: https://www.lancsfirerescue.org.uk/wp-content/uploads/2018/09/personal_emergency_evacuation_plans__peeps_.pdf

SEN Support

As you conduct your regular observations and assessments, you might begin to feel concerned that a child is making little or no progress in the prime areas of the early years foundation stage (EYFS) and suspect they have a special educational need. Together with the SENCO and the child's parents, you might need to make a decision to implement SEN Support.

SEN Support is the name of the support that must be made available to children who have needs which are different from or additional to other children the same age. We tend to believe that it is better to implement intervention strategies to support children sooner rather than later, but this is not necessarily the case. Dorothy Bishop, professor of developmental neuropsychology at the University of Oxford, said in a recent TES Pedagogy podcast, "We see a lot of two-year-olds who are not using as many words, and parents get quite concerned if everybody else's child is chattering away and their child has only got about 20 words...but we know from studies that do follow up that even without any intervention at all, a lot of those children will catch up...you need to look very carefully about who you're intervening with and make sure that you're not just wasting resources by intervening with kids that don't need it".[9]

Unfortunately there are no easy answers about when it is the appropriate time to intervene; it rests on professional experience combined with a knowledge of a particular child and their individual circumstances.

SEN Support is delivered through a personalised and individualised graduated approach. The graduated approach leads to a growing understanding of the child's needs and what support they will need to make good progress. The graduated approach is a four-part cycle: assess, plan, do, review. If a child doesn't make progress after subsequent cycles of the graduated approach, then they may need to be assessed for special educational needs. If a special educational need is identified, then they will be added to your setting's SEN register. When a child is placed on the SEN register the graduated approach still continues.

'Where a pupil is identified as having SEN, schools should take action to remove barriers to learning and put effective special educational provision in place. This SEN support should take the form of a four-part cycle through which earlier decisions and actions are revisited, refined and revised with a growing understanding of the pupil's needs and of what supports the pupil in making good progress and securing good outcomes.'
SEND code, 6.45-6.53

Thorough assessment of the child's needs drives the graduated approach and informs the child's next learning steps. After assessment, a plan is devised for the child and then actioned. After an agreed amount of time this plan is reviewed and the graduated cycle starts again.

High quality teaching forms the basis of the graduated approach. High quality teaching is about having high expectations for all children. It is personalised to individual children's specific needs, stages of development, interests and ways of learning. It is important to reflect on all the different ways that children learn and apply this to your practice.

'The EYFS framework does not prescribe a particular teaching approach. It recognises that effective teaching in the early years requires skilled use of a teaching practice repertoire which responds appropriately to the age and needs of the children being taught.'
Early Years Foundation Stage Reforms: Government consultation, January 2020

The SEND Code says that high quality teaching 'draws on what staff know about children's learning and development, is differentiated for individual children and uses a range of pedagogic approaches'. Learning must be challenging, motivating and enjoyable for all children. The Statutory framework for the foundation stage states that the three characteristics of effective teaching and learning are playing and exploring, active learning and creating and thinking critically.

The SEND Code states that SEN provision **must** be put in place by working 'in partnership with parents to establish the support the child needs' because 'delay at this stage can give rise to learning difficulty and subsequently to loss of self-esteem, frustration in learning and to behaviour difficulties'.

Who is responsible for implementing the graduated approach?

Implementing the graduated approach is your responsibility as a practitioner. You do so by working closely with the SENCO and the child's parent (the term 'parent' means anybody with parental responsibility). It is important to gather the parent's views to ensure the most effective plans are put in place to help the child.

'The graduated approach should be led and coordinated by the setting SENCO working with and supporting individual practitioners in the setting and informed by EYFS materials, the Early Years Outcomes guidance and Early Support resources.'
SEND code of practice, 5.45

The Early Years Outcomes guidance which replaced Development Matters in 2013 is likely to be replaced by a newer version of Development Matters at some point. The 'Early Years Foundation Stage Reforms – Government Consultation' (2020) says, 'There will be an update of the 'Development Matters' guidance'. Early Support is a local authority service that supports children

with special educational needs and their families. When you first implement the graduated approach you will not yet have assessed the child for SEND so Early Support only becomes relevant later. We talk about Early Support later in the chapter.

In Chapter 10, you will find an 'Assess, Plan, Do, Review' form, which you can use to document each graduated cycle, if you wish. Some local authority websites publish their own forms, which you may be able to download and use.

Always give parents copies of completed graduated approach forms. Also provide them with a copy of the early years outcomes so they can see where their child is in relation to the EYFS framework and what the next steps are.

'Practitioners must maintain a record of children under their care as required under the EYFS framework. Such records about their children must be available to parents and they must include how the setting supports children with SEN and disabilities.'
SEND code of practice, 5.50

How do the graduated cycles work?

1. Assess

Together with the SENCO and the child's parents you will make an assessment of the child's needs. The purpose of assessment is to help you to plan an effective learning environment for the child. When carrying out your very first assessment draw upon:

- The experience and views of the child's parents.
- How the child's development compares to that of their peers.
- Your observations and formative assessments against the prime areas in the EYFS.
- Any formal statutory assessments like the progress check at age 2.
- The child's own views (for tips about eliciting children's views see Chapter 5 – 'How can we ensure a young child contributes to their EHCP'). There is also a child's contribution form: 'All About Me' in Chapter 10.

After the first assessment, fill in an 'Initial Record of Concern' form (you will find a form in Chapter 10). This form can be updated when/if the child is diagnosed with SEND.

The form will help you to:

- Write a summative assessment which can easily be shared with all practitioners involved with the child.
- Consider how to adapt activities and the environment to address the child's needs.
- Make a decision about whether or not a child needs SEN Support.

The form should not be filed away – it is a working document. Its purpose is to communicate the child's needs to everybody who works with them to ensure consistent and appropriate actions are taken.

In later graduated approach assessment cycles other professionals may have become involved with the child. The reports written by education and social care professionals and health clinicians will help to inform your assessments by giving a holistic picture of the child's needs. You might also have the results of 'refined assessments' to give you very specific information about the nature of the child's needs. See 'What happens if the child doesn't make progress after subsequent graduated approach cycles?' on page 52.

2. Plan

This is when the strategies, reasonable adjustments and intervention programmes for the child are planned by the SENCO and you in consultation with the child's parents. Strategy ideas are listed under different conditions in Chapter 1 and you can use these even before a child has been diagnosed with SEND. 'Reasonable adjustments' are discussed under the Equality Act 2010 in Chapter 2, and intervention programmes are in a table in Chapter 10. It is very important to work in partnership with parents so they can reinforce strategies and interventions at home.

When you plan support you 'should take into account the views of the child' (SEND code of practice, 5.40). Use the child's interests as a vehicle for learning so that you maximise their engagement and achievement potential. The discussion between you and the SENCO should focus on ways you can adapt the resources and utilise the manpower you already have at your disposal to meet the child's needs. You need to think about the expected impact on the child's progress and a date should be set for review.

If a child is placed on the SEN register the setting will be able to access extra funding from the local authority and then extra support can be put in place (see the SENIF fund in Chapter 9). At this point the SENCO should record interventions on a provision mapping system (see Chapter 10 for a Sample Provision Map), and a date for review should be set to evaluate the effectiveness of each outcome. If a particular intervention is not working for the child you will need to consider whether:

- The intervention can be adapted to make it effective or a different strategy should be put in place.
- The child is using and applying the skills they are learning through targeted intervention.

'The support and intervention provided should be selected to meet the outcomes identified for the child, based on reliable evidence of effectiveness, and provided by practitioners with relevant skills and knowledge. Any related staff development needs should be identified and addressed.' SEND code of practice, 5.40

In Chapter 10 you will find an 'Additional Support Plan' to help you organise the 'plan' stage of the process.

3. Do

This is when planned strategies, interventions and reasonable adjustments are put in place to meet the child's needs.

The SEND Code is clear that the person who works directly with the child is responsible for implementing and reviewing the effectiveness of provision. To do this effectively it's important to work closely and collaboratively with all the other professionals involved with the child:

'The early years practitioner, usually the child's key person, remains responsible for working with the child

on a daily basis. With support from the SENCO, they should oversee the implementation of the interventions or programmes agreed as part of SEN support. The SENCO should support the practitioner in assessing the child's response to the action taken, in problem solving and advising on the effective implementation of support.' SEND code of practice, 5.42

In the 'do' stage you will gain a growing understanding of what strategies work best for the child so you can tailor and hone provision as you go. Ensure that everybody who works with the child maintains high expectations and upholds a commitment to helping them to achieve. The UN Conventions, the Children and Families Act 2014 and the Equality Act 2010 are all very clear about the rights of children with special educational needs and disability and the responsibilities of those who care for them, see Chapter 2.

The 'Do' form in Chapter 10 can be used to help you to record the success of a particular activity. You can write a brief description of the activity, what you would like the child to achieve by the end (the objective), the outcome of the activity and the next steps the child needs to take in order to progress.

4. Review

In the 'review' part of the cycle you and the SENCO will talk to the child's parents in a review meeting to discuss the outcome of the support their child has received and to plan the child's next steps. The child's views must also be taken into account. For tips about how to gather the child's views see Chapter 5 – 'How can we ensure a young child contributes to their EHCP' and you can use the 'All About Me' form in Chapter 10 to record the child's views. Once the child has been diagnosed with SEND other professionals will attend the meeting too. In Chapter 10 you will find a 'Record of Meeting' template which can be a useful tool to have during the 'assess' step.

If parents cannot attend the review meeting make sure they have copies of all the paperwork, and ask them to comment and sign.

The child's progress should be reviewed termly or more. Discussions should focus on:

- The views of parents, professionals and the child on the success of the special educational needs provision and what the next steps will be.

- Whether special educational provision needs to continue in light of the child's progress, based upon firm evidence.
- Whether the graduated approach needs to take place more often.
- If more specialist assessment is needed (see also the 'Assessment tools and interventions table' in Chapter 10).
- Whether staff need more specialist advice or extra training.
- Whether the child requires more specialist support.
- Whether an Education and Health Care Needs Assessment (EHCNA) needs to take place (more in Chapter 4).

At the meeting, share the following paperwork:

- Graduated approach paperwork.
- Assessment documents including a highlighted copy of the EYFS outcomes so that parents can see where their child is and what the next developmental milestones are.
- A record of the child's views – see the 'All About Me' form in Chapter 10.
- Reports from any other professionals involved with the child.

The actions agreed at the review should feed directly into the next cycle of the graduated approach.

Remember: you don't need to wait until a review meeting to speak to parents or other professionals to evaluate the child's progress and to discuss how strategies can be adapted in light of the child's next steps. It is important to have a flexible, proactive approach, always thinking about what is in the child's best interests.

What happens if the child doesn't make progress after subsequent graduated approach cycles?

If a child isn't progressing, or is progressing very little, after successive cycles of the graduated approach you and the SENCO will need to discover whether they have a special educational need. There is no guidance about how many cycles of the graduated approach you need to implement before deciding to assess a child for SEND - you and the SENCO need to use your professional judgement.

The first step is for the SENCO to make sure that factors other than having a special educational need are not causing the child to fall behind their peers. They need to ask themselves:

- How often does the child attend the setting? If they have missed a lot of sessions this could be a reason they are falling behind in one or more of the prime areas. Attendance data may need to be analysed.
- Are there any other factors which could be inhibiting the child's progress? (eg. domestic circumstances).
- Has the child received high quality teaching? How does the setting analyse whether or not teaching approaches are effective for individual children?
- Has assessment data been effectively used to inform planning?
- Have the parent's and child's views been properly considered during the planning process?

Once the SENCO is satisfied that there are no other factors in play, the child themselves will need to be more fully assessed by using refined assessment tools and by involving external professionals.

1. Carrying out refined assessments

There are different assessment tools available to help you establish the specific nature of the child's needs. See the 'Assessment tools and intervention programmes' table in Chapter 10. Some of these tools are free and others cost money.

2. Involving professionals and multi-agency services

You need a parent's permission to ask outside professionals, such as an educational psychologist and a speech and language therapist, to assess their child. If a parent refuses you cannot take this any further. However, if you believe their decision will seriously impair their child's development you can log your concerns under child protection.

At the same time ask parents to talk to their GP or health visitor about your concerns. They might refer the child to a paediatrician to rule out possible health conditions which may be impacting their learning and development.

To involve outside professionals you need to contact your local authority's Early Support team and fill in an Early Help Assessment (EHA) form. Early Support is known by different names in different areas. To find your local service type 'early support' and your area into the search engine or ring your local authority's customer services, to point you in the right direction (see 'Early Support and Early Help Assessment (EHA) on page 54).

'Where there is little or no improvement in the child's progress, more specialist assessment may be called for from specialist teachers or from health, social services or other agencies beyond the setting. Where professionals are not already working with the setting, the SENCO should contact them, with the parents' agreement.'
SEND code of practice, 5.39

Multi-agency professionals could include:

- Specialist teaching services (eg. educators qualified to work with children who have specific difficulties like communication difficulties or visual impairments).
- Educational psychologists.

- Child and Adolescent Mental Health Services (CAMHS).
- Therapists such as physiotherapists, occupational therapists or speech therapists.
- Help from a specialist hearing or visual impairment service.

We talk about the roles of professionals in Chapter 6.

What resources are available within SEN Support?

SEN Support might include specialist intervention programmes and help from outside professionals. To be eligible to receive support from the setting's SEND budget (the SENIF – see Chapter 9 for more) a child needs to be on the setting's SEN register. Staff may need to receive extra training from the budget to meet the child's needs.

SEN Support is likely to involve:

- One-to-one assistance and small group support from early years practitioners.

- Targeted intervention programmes (for examples of intervention programmes see the 'Assessment tools and intervention programmes' table in Chapter 10). Your setting needs to keep track of the effectiveness of intervention programmes through a provision mapping system (more about provision mapping in Chapter 4).
- Support from relevant professionals and multi-agency services (see 'Involving professionals and multi-agency services' on page 53).

All staff working with the child need to understand the child's needs and know what support has been put in place to ensure they meet their learning outcomes.

About Early Support and Early Help Assessments (EHAs)

Early Support is a department within your local authority (it may be known by a different name in your area like 'Early Help'). The department is responsible for providing services for children with SEND in the early years.

To determine the child's and the family's needs, Early Support carry out an Early Help Assessment (EHA). Anybody involved with the child can request an EHA, but you will need the parent's permission if you decide to submit an application.

If you would like to see an example of an EHA and instructions about completing one, see the Cambridgeshire County Council website: https://www.cambridgeshire.gov.uk/residents/children-and-families/parenting-and-family-support/providing-children-and-family-services-how-we-work

Remember that forms vary between local authorities.

After Early Support have determined what support is required, they put in place a family support plan. Meetings then take place between multi-agency professionals and family members to ensure that everyone is working together to meet the child and family's needs. Support will also be provided for transitions – for example if the child moves to a different setting or they are starting school.

What if the child needs more help than Early Support can provide?

At the 'review' stage of the graduated approach cycle it might be agreed that the child needs more support than the setting's SEN Support budget allows in order to make progress. They may, for example, need more one-to-one adult support in the setting or specialist equipment to be able to access the Early Years Foundation Stage (EYFS) curriculum. In this case the SENCO or the child's parents can apply to the local authority for an Education and Health Care Needs Assessment (EHCNA) to discover whether the child is eligible for an Education, Health and Care Plan (EHCP).

A main advantage of having an EHCP is that it gives the child access to fuller SEN provision. In addition, an EHCP is a legal document which means if the provision agreed in the EHCP is not provided by the local authority, the local authority can be taken to a First-tier Tribunal. For more about EHCNAs and EHCPs see Chapters 4 and 5.

Managing transitions

If a child is starting school or moving to a new setting it is a good idea to fill in a transition form to pass on. Some local authorities provide templates on their websites. In Chapter 10 you will find a transition form: 'SEND: Early Years Transition'. On this form you can communicate:

- Whether the child is on SEN Support or has an EHCP.
- The child's levels across each of the prime areas of learning.
- The child's areas for development.
- Effective day-to-day strategies that you use in the setting.
- Anything else you think the new setting/school needs to know – adaptations to the environment, equipment etc.

There is only so much information that can be communicated on a form, so it is best if you and the SENCO meet face-to-face with the child's parents, staff from the new setting, and other professionals involved with the child. By meeting, you can discuss the child's interests, likes and dislikes, fears, and routines – everything the new setting needs to know to ensure a smooth transition.

You also need to help prepare the child themselves for transition. Transition is likely to involve a lot of forward planning and the participation of parents. It is a good idea to start the transition process as soon as possible so that the child feels safe and comfortable before they start. This will involve:

- The child visiting the new setting. This enables the practitioners/teachers to observe the child for themselves and gain a fuller picture of them as well as giving the child an opportunity to build new relationships.
- Parents visiting the new setting. When parents can see what's on offer they can talk about how their child might respond to different toys and activities and what they might find difficult. This enables practitioners to make adjustments. Parents can provide continuity for their child by passing on familiar objects or books from home.
- Home visits. Most schools carry out home visits for all children before they start Reception, and early years settings should be encouraged to do the same. It enables professionals to mirror aspects from the home that will work in the setting.
- Making a book for the child with photographs of themselves and their family in the new setting. Providing pictures of the new setting enables you and the child's parents to talk about it with the child.
- Training. The new setting will need to consider whether their staff have the skills needed to care for the child, and to make sure staff are fully trained before the child starts. See Chapter 10: Resources and Training.

'SEN support should include planning and preparing for transition, before a child moves into another setting or school. This can also include a review of the SEN support being provided or the EHC plan. To support the transition, information should be shared by the current setting with the receiving setting or school. The current setting should agree with parents the information to be shared as part of this planning process.'
Early years: guide to 0-25 SEND code of practice, p.16

Education, Health and Care Needs Assessment (EHCNA)

If despite providing SEN support for a child, they are making insufficient or no progress and your setting is unable to provide the support they need, then it is time to ask the local authority for an Education and Health Care Needs Assessment (EHNCA) - also known as an 'EHC assessment'.

The Children and Families Act, Section 36 (2) defines an EHCNA as '*an assessment of the educational, health care and social care needs of a child*'. The EHCNA is a legal process carried out by the local authority and it is the first step to getting an Education and Health Care Plan (EHCP) put in place for the child. We talk about EHCPs in the next chapter.

Note that the term 'parent' used in this chapter means anybody who has parental responsibility for the child.

It is **very important** to understand that the entire EHCNA and EHCP process follows timescales that are set out by law – see 'Statutory Timescales' (see page 60). For a clarity about timescales also see 'EHCNA and EHCP Timescales' and 'EHCP Review Timescales' in Chapter 10.

When can an EHCNA or 'EHC needs assessment' be requested?

If you have carried out the graduated approach over a period of time and you believe that the child has still not made expected progress, this is the time to request an EHCNA or 'EHC needs assessment' from the local authority.

'A request (for an EHCNA) is likely to happen where special educational provision currently being made for them (the child) by their early years setting, school or college from their own resources, is not enabling the child…to make adequate progress.'
SEND code of practice, 4.57

Once everybody is in agreement (parents, any external professionals involved with the child, such as speech and language therapists, and the manager and SENCO of your setting) then an application for an EHCNA can be made.

The SENCO will contact the local authority to apply for an EHCNA.

In the application form, the SENCO will describe all the actions your setting has taken to meet the child's special educational needs.

They will need to provide evidence of what has already been done to support the child, as well as a description of their concerns and perceptions of the child's needs. They will need to be clear that the child's needs cannot be met through your setting's ordinary SEN support system.

Information about applying for an EHCNA can be found on your local authority's local offer website. Section 30 (9) (a) of the Children and Families Act 2014 states that the local authority's local offer must include 'information about how to obtain an EHC needs assessment'.

Some local authorities publish downloadable EHCNA application forms on their websites which you can print and send, such as this one from Telford & Wrekin Council: https://www.telfordsend.org.uk/download/downloads/id/1158/ehc_needs_assessment_request_form_and_guidance_for_educational_settings.pdf

When applying, remember that 'an EHC needs assessment will not always lead to an EHC plan.

The information gathered during an EHC needs assessment may indicate ways in which the school... or other provider can meet the child or young person's needs without an EHC plan.'
SEND code of practice, 9.6

Who can request an EHCNA from the local authority?

Anybody can bring a child who has, or may have, SEN to the attention of the local authority (SEND Code, 9.9).

However, the only people who can ask the local authority for an EHCNA are the child's parents, or, alternatively, a person acting on behalf of the setting (SEND code of practice, 9.8).

An EHCNA cannot go ahead without the consent of those who have parental responsibility for the child: 'In making a determination under subsection (3), the local authority must consult the child's parent'- Children and Families Act Section 36(4).

When considering whether to carry out an EHCNA local authorities **must**:

- Notify the child's parent that it is considering whether an EHCNA is needed as soon as possible after the request is received. This is so the parent has 'sufficient time to provide their views' – SEND code of practice, 9.12.
- 'Have regard to the views, wishes and feelings of the child and his or her parent,' - SEND code of practice, 9.12. The SEND Code makes it clear that the local authority must proactively involve parents and children in the decision-making process and provide them with all the information and advice they need.

'At an early stage, the local authority should establish how the child and his or her parent…can best be kept informed and supported to participate as fully as possible in decision-making. The local authority must arrange for the child and his or her parent or the young person to be provided with advice and information relevant to the child or young person's SEN.'
SEND code of practice, 9.12

The advice and support for parents will come from the local authority's Special Educational Needs and Disabilities Information, Advice and Support Service (IASS) which can also be called SENDIASS or SENDIAS. IASS provides impartial advice and support for parents. It is very important that parents have the contact details of IASS (or the equivalent service in your area).

How do the local authority decide whether or not to carry out an EHCNA?

When considering whether or not to conduct an EHCNA the local authority will apply the statutory tests described in Section 36(8) of the Children and Families Act 2014:

'The Local Authority will undertake an EHC assessment where it is of the opinion that: (a) the child or young person has or may have special educational needs, and (b) it may be necessary for special educational provision to be made for the child or young person in accordance with an EHC plan.'

The SEND Code, is also very clear about the duties of the local authority:

'A local authority **must** conduct an assessment of education, health and care needs when it considers that it may be necessary for special educational provision to be made for the child…in accordance with an EHC plan.'
Paragraph 9.3

'In considering whether an EHC needs assessment is necessary, the local authority **should** consider whether there is evidence that despite the early years provider… having taken relevant and purposeful action to identify, assess and meet the special educational needs of the child.. (the child) has not made expected progress'.
Paragraph 9.14

Notice the use of 'must' and 'should'. 'Must' is a legal obligation, whereas 'should' is a recommendation.

The SEND code of practice, 9.16, permits local authorities to develop their own criteria for deciding whether or not to undertake an EHCNA. Under this paragraph, local authorities 'must not apply a 'blanket' policy to particular groups of children' and **must** take into account 'individual circumstances'. Local authorities must be prepared to depart from the criteria they have developed 'where there is a compelling reason to do so'.

As a general rule, local authorities use the following indicators to decide whether or not an EHCNA is needed.

1. Developmental milestones

Evidence has been supplied to show that the child has one or more of the following needs:

- Cognition and learning
- Communication and language
- Physical and/or sensory
- Social, emotional and mental health.

Assessment evidence will be needed to prove that the child has not reached the developmental milestones in several or all of these areas, in spite of the graduated approach (see number 2, below). The application will need to include Early Years Foundation Stage (EYFS) assessments and any key progress checks undertaken (such as the progress check at age two). In the application, the SENCO will need to specify a primary area of need and rank other areas in order of priority.

Evidence will show that the child's needs are not changing over time, and that they require extra support to include them in the life of the setting and to develop their independence skills.

2. Barriers to learning and the graduated approach

Evidence will show that every effort has been made to remove barriers to learning and that successive cycles of the graduated approach have taken place actively involving the parent and, as far as possible, the child themselves. For more about removing barriers to learning see Chapter 7, and for the graduated approach read Chapter 3. The local authority will take into account the quality of the graduated approach that has been implemented by the setting. Evidence will show if the child has not progressed, or if they have because the setting has provided 'additional intervention and support over and above that which is usually provided' (SEND code of practice, 9.14).

The local authority will need to be satisfied that the setting has taken every possible action to meet the child's special educational needs and disabilities, including making 'reasonable adjustments to remove or reduce barriers to learning', as detailed in the Equality Act 2010 (refer back to the 'Equality Act 2010' in Chapter 2).

3. Specialists from across education, health and social care

The application will need to include evidence from qualified outside specialists such as (but not limited to) educational psychologists, specialist learning and behaviour support service, teachers of hearing/ visual impairment, speech and language therapists, occupational therapists and physiotherapists. It will need to be clear that qualified specialists have contributed to the setting's interventions and have provided reports about what has taken place and the outcomes. Here the SENCO can include the most recent reports from professionals across education, health and social care.

'Evidence of the child or young person's physical, emotional and social development and health needs, drawing on relevant evidence from clinicians and other health professionals and what has been done to meet these by other agencies. SEND code of practice, 9.14'.

4. Budget

All maintained schools and maintained nurseries are expected to fund up to £6,000 to support children with special educational needs - Schools and Early Years Finance Regulations, 2018, Section 11[10]. Evidence will

need to show that your setting has used its SEND budget fully and appropriately to provide support for the child but the money isn't sufficient. See Chapter 9 for information about government funding for children with SEND.

The setting's evidence of budget usage will most likely be in the form of a fully costed provision map. For an example of a provision map see Tameside Metropolitan Borough's template: https://www.tameside.gov.uk/sen/ Provision-Map-Template.pdf and Northamptonshire's provision mapping tools: https://www3.northamptonshire. gov.uk/councilservices/children-families-education/ early-years/information-for-childcare-providers/the-early-years-curriculum/Pages/special-education-needs-and-inclusion-in-the-early-years-foundation-stage.aspx

At the end of this book, in Chapter 10, you will also find a 'Sample Provision Map' for a child who requires an EHCNA.

Early years settings aren't required to have a provision map, but the SEND code of practice, 6.76, recommends them for helping keep an overview of programmes and interventions for different groups of children. The provision map should cover provision for children with all kinds of additional needs.

Chapter 4: Education, Health and Care Needs Assessment (EHCNA)

Sometimes the local authority will consider an EHCNA when there is not enough evidence to support one. Reasons for this might be that the child has:

- Moved from another local authority where an EHCNA was already in progress.
- Moved from another country but there is clear evidence of severe and complex difficulties.
- Suffered a sudden illness that has caused significant, enduring special educational needs.

The local authority can only make a decision based on the information it receives.

How do I complete an EHCNA application?

In most cases, it is the SENCO who completes the paperwork with the child's parents, the practitioner who works with the child and specialists from across education, health and social care.

EHCNA application forms vary between local authorities. In some areas applications need to be submitted online and in others they must be printed and posted. As an example, see Cambridgeshire's form: https://www.cambridgeshire.gov.uk/residents/children-and-families/local-offer/education-health-and-care-plan-ehcp/

When applying for an EHCNA it is a good idea for the SENCO to have all the documents they need for the application ready because many local authority systems don't allow users to save applications halfway through. In such case, if something is missing, hours of hard work can be lost!

The EHCNA guidelines on the local authority page should list the documents required, but if in doubt your local authority's Special Educational Needs and Disabilities Information, Advice and Support Service - IASS (or your local authority equivalent) can be contacted. The indicators 1-4 on pages 58 and 59, give a general idea of the paperwork needed.

When the SENCO gathers all the information and paperwork to send to the local authority, they should make a copy, just in case anything goes missing.

Statutory Timescales

The Children and Families Act 2014, Special Educational Needs and Disability Regulations 2014, and the SEND code of practice: 0-25 years, set out legal timescales for the entire EHCNA and EHCP process. In Chapter 10 you will find two tables:

- EHCNA and EHCP Timescales
- EHCP Review Timescales.

These two tables will explain exactly what should happen, when it should happen as well as who is responsible for coordinating the actions. They will also specify where in legislation these timescales can be found. It is vital for everyone involved in the EHCNA/EHCP process to have a copy of the timescales, as this will ensure that reports are delivered, collated and sent on time.

When will I know the outcome of the EHCNA?

Once the local authority receives a request for an EHCNA they start analysing the EHCNA application evidence. The local authority has 6 weeks to decide whether or not to carry out an EHCNA:

'The local authority must make a decision and communicate the decision to the child's parent…within 6 weeks of receiving the request… The local authority must also notify the other parties (professionals across health, care and social services, where a child attends an early years setting, the manager of that setting) of its decision.' SEND code of practice, 9.11

Exceptions may apply if:

'(a) exceptional circumstances affect the child, the child's parent…during that 6 week period;

(b) the child, the child's parent or the young person are absent from the area of the authority for a continuous period of not less than 4 weeks during that 6 week period;

or

(c) the child…fails to keep an appointment for an examination or a test made by the body during that 6 week period.'
Special Educational Needs and Disability Regulations 2014, Section 8 (2)

Once a decision has been reached the SEND Code states that the local authority **must** inform the child's parent of their decision. They **must** also inform the health service, social care officers within the local authority, the SENCO and the manager of the setting or the headteacher.

What happens if the local authority decides against carrying out an EHCNA?

If the local authority decides against carrying out an EHCNA they must notify the child's parent of the reasons for their decision:

'The local authority must give its reasons for this decision where it decides not to proceed' - SEND code of practice, 9.17.

The local authority must also inform parents of:

'(a) their right to appeal that decision;

(b) the time limits for doing so;…'
The Special Educational Needs and Disability Regulations, Section 5 (3)

Under the Children and Families Act 2014 (Section 51) parents have a right to appeal the decision to the First-tier Tribunal subject to mediation, and the local authority **must** inform them of this right. The local authority **must** also ensure that parents are aware of the 'availability of information, advice and support' – SEND code of practice, 9.19.

What happens in an EHCNA?

At the very least the local authority must gather educational, medical, and social care advice about the child by collating information from:

- The child's parents and the child themselves
- The SENCO or manager of the setting
- Health and social care professionals
- An educational psychologist.

For more about the evidence local authorities must collate see the Special Educational Needs and Disability Regulations 2014, Section 6: http://www.legislation.gov.uk/uksi/2014/1530/regulation/6/made

A multi-agency meeting will take place to discuss what steps must be taken to address the child's needs, the resources needed and whether or not an EHCP must be put in place. The child and their parents are the centre of the meeting and their views are paramount.

Parents can invite somebody to attend the meeting with them for support. This can be a friend, a family member or somebody from their local Special Educational Needs and Disabilities Information, Advice and Support Service (IASS) team. The Independent Provider of Special Education Advice (IPSEA) is also a source of independent information, advice and support for parents (the website link is in Chapter 10).

Coronavirus implications

The coronavirus pandemic may give your local authority flexibility regarding special educational provision and statutory timescales. See Chapter 2: Legislation, Policies and Procedures, under the title, 'Coronavirus: keeping up-to-date with legislation'.

Education, Health and Care Plan (EHCP)

After carrying out an EHCNA, the local authority may decide that an EHCP must be put in place for the child. An EHCP is a legal document that describes a child's special educational, health and social care needs, the provision that will be put in place to meet these needs, and the planned outcomes. Plans can start as early as birth and can continue as long as needed up until the person is 25 years old.

As in the last chapter, the term 'parent' used in this chapter means anybody who has parental responsibility for the child.

The Children and Families Act 2014

EHCPs and EHCNAs came about as a result of the Children and Families Act 2014. As you read on, you will find it useful to refer back to Chapter 2, since the Act is woven into the whole process.

The Children and Families Act 2014 is clear that parents and children are at the centre of all SEN support. Professionals must focus on the best possible outcomes for children with SEND by:

- Recognising the importance of the wishes, views and feelings of children and their parent.
- Promoting the parent's and child's participation in decision-making.
- Recognising the importance of providing information and support to families. This means that parents and children, as far as possible, must be involved throughout the process. Their feelings, aspirations and wishes, as well as the outcomes they hope to achieve, must be taken into account when planning support.

There are clear requirements set out in the Act. These are regarding:

- Who is involved in the assessment and planning process and when and how this takes place.
- How a child's needs are assessed.
- The content of an EHCP and how it is finalised.
- Timings for the overall process and for the different stages of the assessment and planning process.
- Which decisions of the local authority parents can appeal.
- How EHCPs are maintained and kept under review.

Note that the EHCP and EHCNA process follows timescales that are set out by law.

For more information about the timescales of the process, see 'EHCNA and EHCP Timescales' and 'EHCP Review Timescales' in Chapter 10.

How does the local authority decide whether the child needs an EHCP?

The factors a local authority **should** take into account in deciding whether an EHCP is necessary are set out in paragraphs 9.54 to 9.55 of the SEND code of practice:

'In deciding whether to make special educational provision in accordance with an EHC plan, the local authority **should** consider all the information gathered during the EHC needs assessment and set it alongside that available to the local authority prior to the assessment' – paragraph 9.54.

The local authority **should** also consider whether the special educational needs provision that the setting has made for the child is 'well matched to the SEN of the child' – paragraph 9.54

'Where, despite appropriate assessment and provision, the child or young person is not progressing, or not progressing sufficiently well, the local authority should consider what further provision may be needed…whether it may be necessary for the local authority to make special educational provision in accordance with an EHC plan' - paragraph 9.55.

What happens next?

'Where, in the light of an EHC needs assessment, it is necessary for special educational provision to be made in accordance with an EHC plan, the local authority must prepare a plan.

Where a local authority decides it is necessary to issue an EHC plan, it must notify the child's parent…and give the reasons for its decision.

The local authority should ensure it allows enough time to prepare the draft plan and complete the remaining steps in the process within the 20-week overall time limit within which it must issue the finalised EHC plan' SEND code of practice, 9.53

If the local authority decides not to issue an EHCP and parents wish to appeal, they can take the same steps as if they were refused an EHCNA (see Chapter 4).

Draft EHCP

A draft EHCP is fully written, but it is still open for negotiation and changes. The local authority prepares the draft based upon the information gathered so far in consultation with the child's parent and all the professionals involved. The SENCO will write the information relating to the child's education, and other professionals will write their relevant sections.

The Council for Disabled Children have produced 'good practice' EHCP resources which will help you to understand how SENCOs contribute towards effective EHCPs: https://councilfordisabledchildren.org.uk/help-resources/resources/education-health-and-care-plans-examples-good-practice

The child and their parent also contribute to the draft EHCP:

'Local authorities must consult the child and the child's parent or the young person throughout the process of assessment and production of an EHC plan. They should also involve the child as far as possible in this process. The needs of the individual child and young person should sit at the heart of the assessment and planning process.

Chapter 5: Education, Health and Care Plan (EHCP)

Planning should start with the individual and local authorities must have regard to the views, wishes and feelings of the child, child's parent or young person, their aspirations, the outcomes they wish to seek and the support they need to achieve them. It should enable children, young people and parents to have more control over decisions about their support including the use of a Personal Budget for those with an EHC plan.'
SEND code of practice, 9.2

Section 38 of the Children and Families Act 2014 is clear that when the local authority is preparing the draft EHCP it 'must consult with the child's parent…about the content of the plan during the preparation of a draft of the plan'.

Section 11 states that when preparing a child's EHCP the local authority must:

'(a) take into account the evidence received when securing the EHC needs assessment; and

(b) consider how best to achieve the outcomes to be sought for the child or young person.'

Once the draft is written, the local authority must send copies to the child's parents and the child's educational setting, informing them of the date by which they must submit any requests for changes.

There is a statutory requirement that the plan is finalised within 20 weeks of the request for an EHCNA.

What information should the EHCP contain?

The draft plan will include comprehensive information about the child's special educational, health and social care needs, the provision required to meet those needs and the outcomes that should be achieved as a result of the provision. It will also record the child's feelings, views and aspirations.

Each local authority has its own particular EHCP format, but essentially EHCPs contain the same information because this is set by law:

'Section A: The views, interests and aspirations of the child and his or her parents or the young person.

Section B: The child or young person's special educational needs.

Section C: The child or young person's health needs which are related to their SEN.

Section D: The child or young person's social care needs which are related to their SEN or to a disability.

Section E: The outcomes sought for the child or the young person. This should include outcomes for adult life. The EHC plan should also identify the arrangements for the setting of shorter term targets by the early years provider, school, college or other education or training provider.

Section F: The special educational provision required by the child or the young person.

Section G: Any health provision reasonably required by the learning difficulties or disabilities which result in the child or young person having SEN. Where an Individual Health Care Plan is made for them, that plan should be included.

Section H1: Any social care provision which must be made for a child or young person under 18 resulting from section 2 of the Chronically Sick and Disabled Persons Act 1970: http://www.legislation.gov.uk/ukpga/1970/44/section/2

Section H2: Any other social care provision reasonably required by the learning difficulties or disabilities which result in the child or young person having SEN. This will include any adult social care provision being provided to meet a young person's eligible needs (through a statutory care and support plan) under the Care Act 2014.

Section I: The name and type of the school, maintained nursery school, post-16 institution or other institution to be attended by the child or young person and the type of that institution (or, where the name of a school or other institution is not specified in the EHC plan, the type of school or other institution to be attended by the child or young person).

Section J: Where there is a personal budget, the details of how the personal budget will support particular outcomes, the provision it will be used for including any flexibility in its usage and the arrangements for any direct payments for education, health and social care. The special educational needs and outcomes that are to be met by any direct payment must be specified.

Section K: The advice and information gathered during the EHC needs assessment must be attached (in appendices). There should be a list of this advice and information.'
SEND code of practice, 9.62

How can we ensure a young child contributes to their EHCP?

The child must contribute as much as they can to their EHCP:

'Decisions about the content of EHC plans should be made openly and collaboratively with parents, children and young people. It should be clear how the child… has contributed to the plan and how their views are reflected in it.'
SEND code of practice, 9.61

There are many different ways to elicit young children's views so you can choose the best method for a particular child:

- Augmentative and Alternative Communication (AAC). This form of communication can involve no resources so it might be through sign language and gestures; it might involve resources that are non-technical such as the Picture Exchange Communication System (PECS) in which children communicate through pictures, photographs or symbols; or it could be communication that relies on technology. For more visit, https://communicationmatters.org.uk/.
- The child can draw pictures which can be discussed and annotated.
- Guided walk. The child takes you for a walk around the setting talking about activities they enjoy and do not enjoy. They could take photographs which they could discuss with you later.
- Metaphors. Children use sounds, colours and

textures to communicate. They might scratch sandpaper to communicate discomfort or clap to signal that they like something.
- Rating scales. Smiley, neutral and sad faces or red/amber/green traffic light systems are a quick way to gauge opinions.

In Chapter 10 you will find a Child Contribution form and a Parent View form which can be used to record the child's and their parents' views although your local authority might have their own forms, so check their website first.'

How should EHCP outcomes be written?

An outcome is defined as the difference made to a person's life as a result of an intervention.

'EHC plans must specify the "outcomes sought for the child or young person". Outcomes in EHC plans should be SMART…'- SEND code of practice, 9.61.

SMART outcomes are:

- **S**pecific: the outcome is clear and unambiguous – no generalisations.

- **M**easurable: a measureable outcome means that progress can be quantified. How many? How much? How will I know when it has been achieved?

- **A**chievable: this means the outcome must be within the child's capabilities.

- **R**ealistic: what results can be realistically achieved taking into account the resources available?

- **T**ime-bound: say when the results can be achieved by.

Outcomes can be short-term, medium-term or long-term. There are two types of outcomes, and they can be written together:

- Intrinsic – this is more about personal reward, eg. confidence, happiness and self-esteem.

- Extrinsic – this can be measured by other people and might relate to health or educational achievement, eg. a specific mathematics or literacy target.

Outcomes should be reviewed regularly – not just at the EHCP annual review. Outcomes need to be changed and adapted as and when necessary because children can surprise us in many ways! It is also important to keep checking that interventions are working.

In the EHCP, sections E and F are where outcomes and educational provision are documented. An example of a long-term (12-month) outcome might be: 'Lisa will demonstrate some cooperative play with peers without adult support'. Outcomes should be drawn from 'inspirations' identified in section A of the EHCP. Where appropriate, outcomes should overlap education, health and social care, eg. 'Lisa will continue to develop her self-help skills'.

Short-term outcomes are the stepping stones that lead to long-term outcomes. Short-term outcomes can be documented as an appendix in the EHCP. For example, if a long-term outcome is: 'Emma will demonstrate continued progress in the development of her self-help skills', a short-term outcome linked to this might be: 'Emma will be able to drink from an open cup'.

How can we help parents to review their child's EHCP draft?

The SENCO could set up a joint meeting with parents to look at the draft EHCP together. Here are some ways of supporting parents during the meeting:

1. Encourage parents to check the wording of their child's EHCP to make sure it is very clear. If the wording is unspecific there is a danger their child won't receive high quality provision because professionals won't understand what to do.
2. Give them a copy of the SEND code of practice, sections 9.61, 9.62 and 9.69, as these clearly explain what should be covered in each section of the EHCP.
3. Direct parents to the local authority's local offer, IASS and IPSEA's EHCP checklist or print it out for them: https://www.ipsea.org.uk/Handlers/Download. ashx?IDMF=afd8d11f-5f75-44e0-8f90-e2e7385e55f0
4. Along with the draft EHCP, the local authority should have sent copies of the professional reports that were referred to in the EHCNA. These reports need to be read to check that:

- Nothing is missing that was gathered as part of the EHCNA. If something is missing parents need to contact the local authority.
- The evidence they gave in the EHCNA has been included. It's advisable for parents to go through professional reports highlighting all the special educational needs mentioned and then checking that these have been documented in the EHCP draft.

5. Remind parents that once they receive the draft plan from the local authority they have 15 days to request any changes. If they don't do anything the local authority will go ahead and send them the final plan along with a letter explaining about their right to appeal under the First-tier Tribunal.
6. Refer parents to information about the personal budget (see below).

Personal budget

The local authority will automatically provide funding for the setting to support a child with an EHCP, but parents can also receive direct payments through a personal budget. It is important to make parents aware that the draft EHCP stage is the time when they can request that the local authority set a personal budget for their child. The only other time a local authority will consider setting a personal budget is when an EHCP is reviewed. The legislation surrounding personal budgets can be found in Chapter 2 under the Children and Families Act 2014.

The local authority will only set a personal budget if parents make an explicit request:

'A local authority that maintains an EHC plan, or is securing the preparation of an EHC plan, for a child or young person must prepare a personal budget for him or her if asked to do so by the child's parent or the young person.'
Children and Families Act 2014, Section 49 (1)

The advantage of a personal budget is that it allows parents to make decisions about how money is spent to support their child on the understanding that the money is spent to help the child meet the outcomes in their EHCP.

Parents could spend the money on:

- Meeting the child's educational needs by paying for a specialist therapy or intervention.
- Social care. If the child needs intensive support at home money could be spent on respite care for parents or breaks for the child and their siblings. The aim is to ensure the family has, as far as possible, the same quality of life as other families.

If a child has a complex, life-limiting and long-term health condition they can apply for an NHS health budget which is separate from the 'personal budget'. For more about the funding available to children and families with SEND see Chapter 9.

The Final EHCP

Sections 39 and 40 of the Children and Families Act 2014 state that the local authority must send the finalised EHCP to the child's parents and also the governing body, proprietor or principal of the institution that is named in the plan.

The final EHCP is a legally binding document. Once in place, the local authority must review the plan every 12 months, starting from the date on which the plan was first made (The Children and Families Act 2014, Section 44). If the child's parent, or the proprietor/governor/principal of the setting requests a review at another time, then the local authority must agree a date for a reassessment.

'During a review or reassessment, a local authority must consult the parent of the child…for whom it maintains the EHC plan.'

A local authority can only stop maintaining and EHCP when:

'(a) the authority is no longer responsible for the child or young person, or

(b) the authority determines that it is no longer necessary for the plan to be maintained.'
Children and Families Act 2014, Section 45

If parents disagree with the local authority's decision they can appeal to the First-tier Tribunal subject to mediation (the same as if their child was turned down for an EHCNA or an EHCP).

Chapter 5: Education, Health and Care Plan (EHCP)

Putting the EHCP into practice in the setting

Once a child has an EHCP you still continue to implement the graduated approach (see Chapter 3). The only difference now is that you will cross-reference the EHCP outcomes in your everyday plans. There will now be more resources available to enable the child to achieve to their full potential, including greater access to:

- One-to-one support from the setting's staff and other professionals.
- Specialist resources and equipment.
- Intervention programmes.
- Training for staff to enable them to meet the child's needs.

An EHCP is a legal document, which means that the provision specified in Section F must be provided by the local authority – it is legally binding. If not, parents can apply to the First-tier Tribunal subject to mediation.

'They (early years providers)… have a duty to… provide the educational support specified in the plan,' Early Years: guide to the 0-25 SEND code of practice, p.20.

EHCP annual reviews

An EHCP must be reviewed at least annually (as set out in the Children and Families Act 2014, Section 44). In a review meeting parents and professionals can meet to discuss how the child is progressing in relation to the outcomes, whether the provision is still relevant to the child's needs, and to make plans for the year ahead. Reviews are normally attended by the child's parents, the SENCO, the child's key worker, and professionals from health and social care who are working with the child and their family.

Although EHCP reviews normally take place every 12 months they can be requested from the local authority at any time if the setting and/or parents believe the EHCP no longer effectively meets the child's needs.

Just as with the EHCNA and EHCP process, each step of the annual review must be completed within a specific period of time, and this is set by law. See 'EHCNA and EHCP Timescales' in Chapter 10.

An annual review will normally take place in the setting although it doesn't have to by law:

'The local authority can request (but not require) an early years setting to convene and hold the review meeting on their behalf. In most cases, reviews should normally be held at the educational institution attended by the child or young person. Reviews are generally most effective when led by the educational institution. They know the child best, will have the closest contact with them and their family and will have the clearest information about progress and next steps. Reviews led by the educational institution will engender the greatest confidence with the child and their family.'
Early Years: guide to the 0-25 SEND code of practice, p.23

Where the child attends a preschool setting other than a maintained nursery school the annual review report is the local authority's responsibility:

'Where the child or young person does not attend a school referred to in paragraph (12), the local authority must prepare a written report on the child or young person, setting out its recommendations on any amendments to be made to the EHC plan, and referring to any difference between those recommendations and recommendations of others attending the meeting.'
Special Educational Needs and Disability Regulations 2014, Section 20 (8)

The person coordinating the annual review (normally the SENCO) should set the meeting date in good time to ensure that as many relevant professionals as possible are able to attend. Annual review invitations must be sent to the child's parent and representatives from education, health and social care services at least two weeks before the meeting. Parents can bring somebody along to support them during the meeting (normally a representative from IASS, but it can be anybody they wish).

The SENCO should request written reports from all the professionals involved with the child and gather the views of the child and parent as soon as possible before the annual review because copies need to be circulated to all those invited at least two weeks beforehand.

Before the annual review meeting, parents and professionals should read the child's EHCP targets carefully so they can talk about what actions to take in view of targets that have been met/unmet.

For children who attend a school or maintained nursery school, an annual review report must be written by the SENCO after the meeting. Each local authority has their own annual review report form, but here is Cambridgeshire's as an example: https://www.cambridgeshire.gov.uk/residents/children-and-families/local-offer/education-health-and-care-plan-ehcp

This report must be submitted to the local authority, the child's parents, and the professionals involved (whether or not they attended the meeting) within two weeks of the annual review meeting taking place.

'The early years setting must prepare and send a report of the meeting to everyone invited within two weeks of the meeting. The report must set out recommendations on any amendments required to the EHC plan, and should refer to any difference between the recommendations of the setting and those of others attending the meeting.'
Early years: guide to 0-25 SEND code of practice, p.23

Once the local authority has received a copy of the annual review report, it is up to them to decide whether any amendments need to be made to the EHCP in light of what has been discussed. Once the parent receives the local authority's response they have 15 working days to respond if they disagree with any of the proposed changes. Just as with the rest of the EHCP process, parents have a right to appeal if they disagree with decisions made about their child.

Transitions and EHCP reviews

If a child already has an EHCP and they are moving from one setting to another (or from nursery to school) the local authority will contact the new setting before naming it in the child's EHCP.

When a child is transferring between phases of education (such as from nursery to primary school) then an EHCP review meeting must take place within a specific timeframe:

'…where a child…is within 12 months of a transfer between phases of education, the local authority must review and amend, where necessary, the child or young person's EHC plan before— (b) 15 February in the calendar year of the child's transfer in any other case, and where necessary amend the EHC plan so that it names the school…or type of school or institution, which the child…will attend following that transfer.'
Special Educational Needs and Disability Regulations 2014, Regulation 18(1).

Coronavirus implications

The coronavirus pandemic may give your local authority flexibility regarding special educational provision and statutory timescales. See Chapter 2: Legislation, Policies and Procedures under the title, 'Coronavirus: keeping up-to-date with legislation'.

SENCO and multi-agency professionals

All early years providers that are funded by the local authority must have a Special Educational Needs Coordinator (SENCO). It is the SENCO's role to support practitioners to develop high-quality, inclusive teaching for all children with special educational needs and disability (SEND).

It is also the SENCO's role to co-ordinate the setting's response to children with SEND, which means collaborating with parents and other education, health and social care professionals to ensure effective provision is put in place.

There are a number of professionals who play a key role in special educational provision. They advise, assess and treat a child in order to give them every chance to realise their full potential. Every professional is a vital part of the puzzle, and in this chapter we talk about each of their roles and responsibilities.

The role and responsibilities of the SENCO

In maintained nursery schools, the SENCO must be a member of staff who is holding the Qualified Teacher Status (QTS). They will also be required to gain a National Award for Special Educational Needs Co-ordination within three years of taking the post. Other early years providers must have a SENCO qualified to at least Level 3.

Childminders normally fulfil the role themselves, although if they are part of a network or agency they can share the role between them (Early Years Foundation Stage Statutory Framework (EYFS), paragraph 3.67).

The SENCO needs to understand the key legislation which underpins their role - see Chapter 2.

The SENCO works in partnership with practitioners, the setting manager, parents and other multi-agency professionals effectively, to ensure that all children in the setting's benefit from the highest standard of early years provision, and that families receive the support they need in order for their children to thrive. So their responsibilities include making parents aware of sources of support available to them both locally, as set out on the local authority's 'local offer' website (see 'The local offer' in Chapter 2), and nationally, usually through charitable organisations (see Chapter 1 and Chapter 10 for useful websites for parents).

The SENCO's role is set out in the SEND code of practice, paragraph 5.54.

SENCO's key responsibilities

- Educate practitioners about their legal responsibilities towards children with SEND (see Chapter 2).
- Lead inclusion in the setting by making sure inclusive values and practices are adopted and make sure all children can access the EYFS curriculum and any extracurricular activities (see Chapter 7).
- Review and update the setting's SEND policy to ensure it is effective, sharing the policy with parents and making sure that all practitioners thoroughly understand and implement it.
- Act promptly when a child isn't making progress, working with the child's key worker, the child and their parents to identify the best provision to enable the child to make progress.
- Support practitioners to develop inclusive, high-quality teaching for all children by monitoring, planning and observing practice. This involves:
  - Ensuring practitioners can identify SEND and have the skills and training to meet individual children's needs through continuous professional development (CPD). This can be through training courses or mentoring by the SENCO themselves or other colleagues.
  - Supporting practitioners to assess children's particular strengths and weaknesses and to use their assessments effectively.
  - Reinforcing to practitioners that they must have high expectations of all children and a commitment to ensuring that every child in their care achieves their best.

- Supporting practitioners to plan and implement the graduated approach (see Chapter 3).
- Monitoring how SEN provision is implemented through observations and then working with practitioners to ensure success.
- Make sure children are assessed effectively and their needs are identified by monitoring the effectiveness of assessments.
- Track the progress of all children with SEND and report to parents, the setting manager and other professionals involved as soon as possible.
- Monitor the effectiveness of provision through a provision mapping system together with the setting manager, considering the SEND budget and value for money.
- Make referrals to multi-agency professionals when needed.
- Request Education, Health and Care Needs Assessments (EHCNA) on behalf of the setting (see Chapter 4).
- Coordinate the EHCP process including review meetings, ensuring all steps take place in a timely manner, in adherence to the law (see Chapter 5).
- Maintain a good relationship with the local authority, understanding how the local authority SEND system works and make full use of the resources available.

Chapter 6: SENCO and multi-agency professionals

- Know what special educational needs and disabilities funding is available (see Chapter 9).
- Evaluate SEND provision under Ofsted's criteria.

The SENCO's role in the graduated approach

The SENCO plays a key role in the graduated approach. The graduated approach is covered in more details in Chapter 3. Here is a summary of how the SENCO is involved in each stage of the cycle:

Assess
Support a child's keyworker to analyse the child's needs taking into account observations, assessments and the views of the child, their parents and all professionals involved with the child.

Make sure that assessments are moderated, so that there is shared agreement about what evidence demonstrates that a child has met a particular outcome.

Plan
Plan effective provision for the child in collaboration with parents, the child's keyworker, and other relevant

professionals, and make sure all practitioners working with the child know what interventions and strategies are in place, so that the child has every chance to meet their outcomes. With regard to intervention programmes, the SENCO must:

- Record provision made for the child on a provision map (see Chapter 10 for a Sample Provision Map).
- Monitor the effectiveness of the provision put in place for the child in an organised and robust manner.

Do
Liaise closely with practitioners who are delivering provision, monitoring the delivery of interventions and strategies. Provide constructive feedback and support to practitioners so that delivery continues to be effective.

Review
Together with the child's keyworker, analyse the impact of additional provision on the child's progress.

Organise graduated approach review meetings with parents, the child's keyworker and other professionals, making sure that meetings focus on the progress the child has made and to what extent their outcomes have been met. Check that everyone attending the meeting will bring evidence with them to support their views and judgements. Make sure that steps agreed upon in the meeting impact the next cycle of the graduated approach and, if applicable, result in an Education and Health Care Needs Assessment (EHCNA) - see Chapter 4.

Working with parents, children, and other professionals

Partnership working is embedded in both the Children and Families Act (2014) and the SEND Code (see Chapter 2). The SENCO is required to collaborate with the child themselves, the child's parents, and outside agencies and professionals in the setting.

The SENCO needs to seek the views of the child in order to devise learning targets. A child's contributions influence the graduated approach and the Education, Health and Care Plan (EHCP) process. In Chapter 5 we talked about methods that can be used to elicit children's contributions. Children and their families are at the centre of SEN Support. Chapters 3, 4 and 5 discuss how to ensure they are the focal point of the graduated approach, the EHCNA and EHCP process.

Developing effective partnerships with families, multi-agency professionals and early years practitioners takes investment and time. It is important for the SENCO (and everybody else) to:

- Be open to challenging existing practice by setting assumptions aside.
- Listen to others' perspectives and value their contributions.
- Be prepared to think in a different way considering others' ideas.
- Be willing to try new approaches and strategies.
- Learn from other people, including other professionals, the child and their parents.

SENCOs need to keep a record of all the health, social and educational professionals that work with each child with SEND and this should be easily accessible. In Chapter 10 we have included a 'Record of Services' form that could be used for this purpose.

The SENCO and the local authority's 'local offer'

The local authority's local offer webpage is designed to be the 'place to go' for SENCOs, practitioners and parents alike. It is where you can find your local authority Area SENCO, as well as local support services tailored to specific needs - Behaviour Support Service, ASD (Autism) Advisory Support Service, Speech and Language Service and more. In short, the local offer details all the education, health and social provision the local authority expect to be available locally for children with SEND and their families.

You might also find referral forms, graduated approach paperwork, practical resources that can be used to support children with SEND, transition guidance, comprehensive EHCP resources and much more.

Unfortunately, local authority websites do vary in quality. Some are more comprehensive and easy to navigate than others. However, the Special Educational Needs and Disability Regulations 2014 specify the requirements that all local authorities must meet in their local offer. The

SEND code of practice, 4.30 also sets out what the local offer must include.

If your local authority's website isn't fit for purpose it is important to bring it to their attention by following their complaints procedure. Complaints can also be made to the Local Government and Social Care Ombudsman: https://www.lgo.org.uk/make-a-complaint/fact-sheets/education/special-educational-needs

It is the SENCO's responsibility to bring the local offer to parents' attention. If your local offer homepage is difficult to navigate, then parents could be provided with a specific link to a service or piece of information they require within the site.

In Chapter 2, under the Children and Families Act 2014, you will find more information under the heading 'Local offer'.

Evaluating SEND provision under Ofsted's criteria

Ofsted's new Education Inspection Framework (EIF), which took effect from September 2019, puts greater emphasis on inspecting SEND provision. Inspectors

judge how effectively children's needs have been identified, assessed and met. Early years settings and schools should have an inclusive culture that complies with legislation (see Chapter 2 and Chapter 7). Managers and leaders should have 'a clear and ambitious vision for providing high-quality, inclusive education to all learners'.

To prepare for an Ofsted inspection, SENCOs will need to read relevant sections in 'Early years: guide to SEND Code 0-25', 'SEND Code of Practice 0-25 years', 'Ofsted Early Years Inspection Handbook 2019', and the 'Education Inspection Framework (EIF)'.

SENCOs must be able to:

- Talk about the processes by which they identify and assess children with SEND.
- Demonstrate how they monitor and manage provision.
- Show that children with SEND meet or exceed their targets, and if not, be able to provide reasons and evidence to explain why not.
- Explain how they manage behavioural, emotional and social difficulties.
- Provide evidence of the ways in which they support practitioners to improve their SEND practice.
- Show how they gather the views of children and parents and use them to inform the graduated approach.
- Talk about how they work with outside professionals.
- Justify how the setting's SEND budget is spent.
- Show that they've read and addressed the SEND action points from the setting's last Ofsted inspection report, and provide evidence to demonstrate what progress has been made.

For more about the changes to the way Ofsted inspects SEND provision see 'Ofsted's education inspection framework: 2019' in Chapter 2.

Where can the SENCO find support?

The SENCO can talk to the Area SENCO (see further below) and seek guidance from a variety of other organisations – see Chapter 10. They can also find guidance, advice and support from the local authority's Special Educational Needs and Disabilities Information, Advice and Support Service (IASS/SENDIASS/SENDIAS). If a child has been diagnosed with a specific special educational need or disability they can seek advice from the associated charity (you will find website links under relevant headings in Chapter 1).

NASEN's SEND gateway is a one-stop website for everything related to SEND. They also host a SENCO forum, for more information visit: https://www.sendgateway.org.uk/whole-school-send/

Equalities Named Co-ordinator (ENCO)

It is good practice for settings to have an ENCO. This person can - but does not have to be - the SENCO too. The Equality Act 2010 places a legal responsibility on settings to eliminate discrimination and promote equality (see Chapter 2). It's the ENCO's role to ensure the setting complies with legislation by identifying inequality and coordinating work to ensure the setting is inclusive (see Chapter 7). To qualify as an ENCO, a practitioner undergoes a three-day training course – contact your local authority education department for more details.

The ENCO's role overlaps with the SENCO, and they should work closely together in order to:

- Raise awareness of the needs of groups vulnerable to prejudice and discrimination with all professionals in the setting, as well as volunteers, parents and children.
- Implement strategies to combat negative behaviour and promote positive attitudes towards others.
- Foster positive relationships with the local community and promote community involvement in the setting.
- Implement and monitor the impact of the setting's Equality Policy.
- Promote a culture in which prejudice is reported and recorded.
- Make sure all staff receive equalities training.
- Review the appropriateness of the language and terms used by staff relating to equalities.
- Ensure that equality and diversity are an integral part of staff recruitment and induction.
- Foster an environment in which staff can ask for advice when they need to.
- Review toys and resources to make sure they reflect diversity in the setting.

- Make sure that parents who speak English as a second language can access information from the setting, such as letters sent home and policies.

Health, social care and educational professionals and multi-agency services

Area SENCO

An early years Area SENCO is an advisory teacher employed by the local authority. Their role includes:

- Providing practical advice and support to practitioners to help them to identify and support children with SEND and to plan strategies and interventions.
- Providing training and support for SENCOs through training sessions, visits and local SENCO district meetings.
- Working closely with educational psychologists in particular, but also with other multi-agency professionals across education, health and social care to support children with SEND and to facilitate transitions to school.
- Working in partnership with parents through visits to early years settings and through multi-agency meetings.
- Informing parents about where they can find more support and advice.
- Attending Education and Health Care Plan (EHCP) review meetings.

The Area SENCO's role is summarised in the SEND code of practice, 5.56.

Educational psychologist

Educational psychologists are healthcare professionals who work with children who have difficulties that prevent them from participating in the everyday activities. Children might have:

- Concentration difficulties.
- Emotional, behavioural, social and physical needs.
- Learning difficulties/learning disabilities.
- Sensory needs, such as problems with hearing or eyesight.

They play a key role in the Education Health and Care Needs Assessment (EHCNA) and work closely with specialist teachers, occupational therapists, physiotherapists, speech and language therapists, early years settings, schools and parents to devise appropriate targets and interventions to accelerate children's progress. Educational psychologists work with children in the setting, but they can also support parents to meet the needs of their child at home.

They can work with children one-to-one and they can provide training for practitioners on areas such as behaviour management, bullying and stress management. They can also advise settings, schools and local authorities about their SEND policies.

Occupational therapist

Occupational therapists are health care professionals who support children with physical, sensory and/or cognitive disabilities and who find daily activities challenging. They aim to help children become as independent as possible to conduct self-care tasks, such as eating, drinking, dressing, toileting and hygiene. They help develop children's fine and gross motor skills and their social skills through purposeful activities and by modifying the environment for better support and participation.

Occupational therapists work with parents and settings by providing advice and showing them how to deliver interventions, one-to-one therapy, and how to conduct risk assessments to make environments safe. They can also make referrals for personal equipment in order to promote a child's independence both at home and in the setting.

Physiotherapist

Physiotherapists are health care professionals who help children affected by injury, illness, disability or developmental delay. They help children to develop mobility skills, muscle strength and motor skills in order that they can become as independent as possible. Working closely with occupational therapists, they give practitioners advice on activities to enable children access the EYFS curriculum. They support children who:

- Are delayed in reaching motor skills milestones.
- Have a diagnosed neurological or rheumatic condition.

- Have problems with balance and coordination which affects the daily living of the child.
- Have deteriorating physical abilities.
- Need rehabilitative treatment following or due to a medical condition or injury.

Children can be seen at home or in the setting. The physiotherapist puts in place a physiotherapy programme of exercises and they may also provide equipment to aid mobility. This programme is given to the parent, and can be shared with the setting and other professionals with the parent's consent.

Speech and Language Therapist (SLT)

They play a vital role in supporting settings to meet the needs of children with speech, language and communication needs (SLCN). They provide individual support and advice, putting in place strategies and interventions for children who have, or are at risk of developing, early language delay (children who are not achieving expected levels in the EYFS). These may include difficulties with understanding verbal language, attention and listening skills, expressive language, vocabulary and word finding, speech sounds, fluency, and voice.

Speech and language therapists also support children with feeding and swallowing difficulties (dysphagia). They support safe eating and drinking by providing direct intervention for children with complex needs.

They also help parents to manage their child's mealtimes as safely as possible.

How educational psychologists, occupational therapists, physiotherapists and speech and language therapists (SLTs) support the setting

These professionals all support the setting by:

- Confirming or identifying that a child has a difficulty.
- Assessing the cause and nature of the difficulty.
- Putting together a treatment plan by talking to the child, the child's parents, the setting and other involved professionals.
- Training practitioners to carry out intervention programmes or programmes of exercise.
- Monitoring and evaluating the child's progress.
- Reviewing the effectiveness of the programme.
- Providing equipment such as walking frames and wheelchairs (occupational therapist and physiotherapist only).
- Working closely with settings to adapt environments and provide appropriate resources and games to help the child.
- Writing reports for annual reviews and attending if enough notice is given.

Child and Adolescent Mental Health Services (CAMHS)

CAMHS is a multi-disciplinary agency made up of professionals including nurses, psychiatrists, psychologists and social workers. They support and treat children who have emotional and behavioural difficulties and their families.

After carrying out an assessment of the child's needs they design a personalised care package with the child's family and other professionals already supporting the child. Signs a child is experiencing difficulties could include:

- Difficulty settling or problems with sleeping.
- Being extremely clingy.
- Toileting problems.
- Being withdrawn.
- Eating difficulties.
- Temper tantrums.

Of course these behaviours can also be perfectly normal. It is down to professional judgement to decide when behaviour is sudden, excessive or age-inappropriate. The cause could be as simple as the birth of a sibling, or it could be an indication that abuse is taking place – see Chapter 8.

Child Development Centre (CDC)

Child Development Centres (CDCs) are found in hospitals. They are assessment centres that provide assessment, treatment and support for children with special educational needs and disabilities. The CDC team includes professionals such as paediatricians, physiotherapists, speech and language therapists, occupational therapists, clinical psychologists, and music therapists. A child can be referred to a CDC by a health professional.

Community paediatrician

Community paediatricians are health professionals who work with vulnerable children and their families. Vulnerable children include those with special educational needs, physical disabilities and complex needs. Community paediatricians play a key role in overseeing children's care, providing medical assessment and referrals to other professionals. They write reports for Education and Health Care Plans (EHCPs).

Dietician

Children with special educational needs and disability are at greater risk of developing conditions related to food, health and dietary needs, such as bowel disorders, oral health problems, diabetes, reflux, swallowing difficulties, and issues with body weight.

Dietitians provide individualised, practical advice for parents to use to ensure their children have a healthy diet and lifestyle. A child is likely to see a Registered Dietician within the NHS after referral from a GP, health visitor or paediatrician.

Reasons a child would benefit from being referred to a dietitian include:

- Poor weight gain and growth.
- Over or under eating to a noticeable degree.
- Poor digestion.
- A condition that affects eating, such as coeliac disease, a food allergy or a metabolic disease.
- Children who have difficulties chewing or swallowing.

When a child has difficulty with chewing or swallowing, a speech and language therapist will help them with the physical difficulty. A dietician becomes involved when a child is losing weight or is underweight for their age.

Health Visitor

Health visitors care for children from when they are ten days old and they can advise families up until their children are five. The health visitor might be the first professional to notice that a child has a developmental delay when they're carrying out their checks.

As well as advising parents, health visitors can also support settings with children who have SEND. A health visitor can make referrals to different professionals and services. Their service is normally delivered in children's or community centres, GP practices or in the home. With the permission of the child's parents, health visitors can also visit the setting to give advice and support, attend family support meetings and contribute to the child's Education, Health and Care Needs Assessment (EHCNA).

Health visitors deliver the government's Healthy Child Programme (HCP): https://www.gov.uk/government/publications/healthy-child-programme-0-to-19-health-visitor-and-school-nurse-commissioning

Hearing and visual impairment services

When children have a hearing or visual impairment, specialist teachers work closely with settings and parents, advising on the most effective ways to help the child. Specialists will:

- Diagnose the impairment.
- Work with other professionals to support the child (early years practitioners, ophthamologists, paediatricians, health visitors, GPs, voluntary organisations, and Early Support).
- Provide specialist hearing or visual impairment equipment.
- Advise and train setting staff to:
  - Use specialist equipment.
  - Adapt resources and the environment so the child can access the EYFS curriculum.
  - Communicate with the child through the use of Braille or sign language programmes, for example.
- Contribute to the child's Education, Health and Care Plan (EHCP) targets.
- Contribute to the child's EHCP annual review and fulfill other statutory assessments.

Orthotist

They prescribe, measure and fit equipment for children with physical disabilities, such as splints, braces and specialist footwear. They work collaboratively with other healthcare professionals, such as physiotherapists and occupational therapists.

If a child has been referred to an orthotist it is important to learn how to use the aids and to know how long the aids have been prescribed for. You may also need to keep a record of any discomfort the child shows when using the aids.

Playworkers/play therapists

Playworkers/play therapists are skilled practitioners who support children with a range of emotional, social, physical and intellectual needs. They enrich and enhance children's play by helping them to make the most of the range play opportunities available to them (role play, dramatic play, block play, messy play etc). Playworkers are a valuable (but scarce!) resource.

Find out more from your local authority and Play England: http://www.playengland.org.uk/playwork-2/.

Social care service/Social worker

By law, local authorities have a responsibility to support children with SEND and their families. They provide this service through their social care department which is sometimes called 'social services', 'children with disabilities team', or 'children's care services'.

When a child has SEND, a social worker will carry out an assessment to find out what the child and their family need to support them, this is called a 'social care assessment' or a 'child in need assessment'. They liaise regularly with other professionals including SENCOs, doctors and police. They will make a plan for the child and their family setting out what kind of help will be provided (child care, home help, essential equipment, short breaks for parents and children etc), how long the help will be available, and what difference the help is expected to make.

Social care is responsible for ensuring children, and their families have access to all the services they require so that they enjoy a standard of living that is (as far as possible) the same as everybody else. Social workers contribute to Education, Health and Care plans (EHCPs). If a child has complex needs, the social worker will attend EHCP review meetings in person.

Parents and early years settings can contact their local authority's social care team at any time to ask for advice about anything concerning a particular child – from behavioural difficulties to access to short breaks for parents.

Specialist teacher

Specialist teachers provide support for children with SEND through home visits and visits to the setting. They support children who have been identified as having SEND after successive graduated approach cycles (regardless of whether they have an EHCP or not). They work alongside practitioners to devise and carry out strategies and intervention programmes tailored to a particular child. They can also provide training for SENCOs, practitioners and parents.

All maintained nurseries have a link to a local authority specialist teacher. To involve a specialist teacher, parental consent must be sought, and then a 'Required Information and Consent' form or Early Help Assessment (EHA) will need to be completed – see your local authority's website.

Specialist practitioner

Specialist practitioners support the work of specialist teachers and educational psychologists. Their work is very similar to the specialist teacher. They may work one-to-one with children in the setting or in the home, and run support groups for parents.

When they work in the setting they share their skills and knowledge over a period of six weeks, so that practitioners can continue to support the child effectively once they have left.

Specialist practitioners are not accessed directly, but through educational psychologists or specialist teachers.

Portage

The National Portage Association defines Portage as 'a home-visiting educational service for preschool children with SEND and their families'. The Portage service is a free service that works closely with families to minimise the barriers that prevent their children and themselves from getting the most out of their lives.

They work with families to raise their quality of life so that they can play together, learn together and participate in their community.

Portage practitioners have a positive 'can do' approach, aiming to empower parents to make informed choices about their child's development. They offer practical strategies, signpost parents towards sources of help, and work together with parents to identify and solve problems.

Not all local authorities have a Portage service. To find out whether there is Portage in your area go to: https://www.portage.org.uk/support/region. Moreover, the nature of the service itself varies between localities depending upon local authority budgets. Usually, they:

- Help families to coordinate their child's care and learning.
- Offer a weekly drop in group where parents can find support and friendship.
- Advise parents on how they can help their child learn through playing together.

- Provide targets to support the child's development.
- Guide parents towards sources of information to help them to develop their knowledge about SEND.
- Support with transition to school.
- Provide an early years inclusion library so that parents can borrow specialist resources and equipment.

If your area does not have Portage, search the internet for your local inclusion service, eg. 'Liverpool early years inclusion'.

Although primarily for families, settings can ring their local Portage (or equivalent) service for SEND advice too.

Removing barriers to learning

Children with special educational needs and disability (SEND) have barriers to learning due to the nature of their condition.

By law every setting must provide all children with an equal chance to achieve their full potential, doing everything possible to remove barriers to learning through inclusive provision and a culture of positivity, inclusion and mutual respect.

All early years practitioners need to be proactive in removing barriers such as stereotyping, bias and negativity. A child with SEND will form a perception of themselves based upon the way others behave towards them. Therefore, positive attitudes must be fostered and embedded in the setting's culture so that all children can grow up feeling valued, confident about who they are, with aspirations to achieve and a life-long love of learning.

The Equality Act 2010 is clear that children with disabilities must not be treated less favourably than their peers and that 'reasonable adjustments' must be made to accommodate them.

Fostering inclusive language and attitudes in the setting

Children are naturally curious and when they see a child who is different in some way they notice and ask about it, so how can you respond positively?

Rather than giving a detailed and emotional explanation, give a short matter-of-fact answer and keep your explanations positive. For example, rather than saying, 'He is in a wheelchair because he can't walk,' you might say: 'Some people's muscles work differently. He needs the wheelchair to help him to move around, just like your legs help you'. If a child has a hearing aid rather than saying: 'She can't hear,' you could say: 'The hearing aid helps her to hear'.

When talking about someone with a disability use words that aren't derogatory. Derogatory terms hurt and will cause the child to feel 'less than' others. Don't use a disability to describe an individual. For instance, say the words '…has Down Syndrome' rather than 'a Down's child'. Read 'Inclusive Language: words to avoid and use when writing about disability' (website link in Chapter 10).

Emphasise similarities between the child with a special educational need or disability and the other children. Help children to understand that, like them, the child enjoys playing and has the same feelings and emotions. What else do they have in common? Do they like the same animals? Do they enjoy swimming or riding a tricycle?

It is important to teach children that disabilities do not define people. Encourage children to notice the child's strengths rather than just their difficulties. Highlight the fact that everybody has their strengths and struggles. Other children in the setting may need help to zip up their coats or put on their wellies, just as another child needs assistance to walk.

An inclusive environment benefits all children. They learn to respect everybody in the setting and to recognise every person's unique abilities. They develop a sense of empathy and learn to provide sensitive support when it is needed.

Toys and books that feature people with disabilities

Dr Amber Hewitt, a psychologist from American University, says it is vital that children play with toys that reflect themselves otherwise they will think the people like them do not matter. "All messages can impact a child's sense of self-worth and can perpetuate stereotypes. It's important to remember that not all messages that children receive are verbal. And children learn, including learning messages about identity, through play."[11]

In the 1940s, psychologists Kenneth and Mamie Clark carried out experiments called 'The Doll Tests'. They showed a group of Afro-American children, aged between three and seven, four dolls that were identical except for their colour. They asked the children what colour doll they preferred and why. Most of the children chose the white doll and described it in positive terms. The experiment demonstrated that bias and a low sense of self-worth is instilled in children from a young age. That's why it is important to think about the messages we communicate to children through the books and toys we give them to play with. We also need to think about how displays on walls, the media and interactive games communicate negative or positive messages.

There are many toys and games available that reflect disabilities. The following websites suggest toys and games that promote inclusion in the early years:

Why you should give kids toys that look like them, MashableUK
https://mashable.com/article/toys-diversity-inclusion/?europe=true

16 books games and toys for kids that feature people with disabilities, The Mighty https://themighty.com/2018/11/kid-toys-disability-representation/

Managing daily activities

Daily routines can present particular challenges for children with special educational needs and disabilities. Social stories are a useful tool for helping children who have specific social difficulties, helping them to make sense of social situations. These stories promote self-awareness, self-calming and self-management (see Chapter 10 for useful websites).

Here we look at some strategies to help at different times of the day.

Outdoor play

The reality is that the outdoor learning environment will include equipment that some children will be unable to use, but there are still plenty of ways that play spaces outside can be made as inclusive as possible.

- Make garden paths and mazes as wheelchair friendly as you can by including some wider paths and even surfaces. In reality, the world is never going to be completely accessible, so it's good for children to learn to work together by asking for and giving help to each other.

- Provide different types of seating. Children with hypersensitivity might prefer to sit on particular kinds of seats.

- Consider children who engage in repetitive, self-stimulating movement activities, such as rocking, spinning round or bumping into people. Include equipment which gives them a similar sensory input, eg. ballpit, swing, space hoppers, large saucers for twirling around.

- Include push/pull toys such as pushchairs and carts, so children with coordination difficulties can use them as walking aids.

- Provide rideon toys, beams and stepping stones, and large equipment like slides and climbing frames, so children can push, pedal, steer, climb and balance.

- Think about creating outdoor areas that evoke children's senses. All children, and especially those with sensory processing disorders, benefit from nature play. Here are some ideas:

  - Mud kitchen with 'recipe' cards that encourage children to create mixtures with sticks, pine cones, grass, lentils, shells, rice leaves etc.

- Digging area. Vary toys and equipment to entice all children, for example toy diggers, cooking utensils, or gardening equipment.

- Sensory garden which encourages children to see, hear smell, touch and (under supervision) taste. Plant child-safe scented herbs, fruits and plants of different textures, sizes and colours. The Royal Horticultural Society school gardening web page is full of ideas. What sounds will children hear in the garden? Water flowing over pebbles? Long grasses blowing in the wind? Wind chimes? Nature Play at Home by Nancy Striniste is an inspirational guide to creating a child-friendly sensory garden.

- Sound stations can be made with pots, pans, pipes, wooden slats, xylophones, and recycled objects.

- Areas where children can view the world from different perspectives including caves, mounds, slopes, tunnels and ditches.

Outings

Outings are important for all children – whether it's a trip to the park, library, museum, theatre or the local shop. Experiencing the world beyond the setting, helps them to develop their understanding of the world, enhances their vocabulary, furnishes them with new experiences that they can bring to their play, improves their social skills, boosts confidence and improves independence.

Outings are a kinaesthetic, visual and sensory learning experience that benefits all children. However, before you venture out you need to consider that for some children with SEND, especially those on the autistic spectrum and who have sensory processing disorders, new environments can be overwhelming. This means advanced planning and preparation is important.

You can prepare the child by:
- Looking at images on websites to show the child where you will be going.
- Showing the child photographs of members of staff who work at the venue.
- Looking at pictures of landmarks you will pass on the journey there.
- Organising a day in the setting where you focus on the place you will be visiting. For example, if you're going to the farm arrange activities around that theme and share sensory stories about it.

- Using social stories to help the child understand any rules they will need to obey when they get there, eg. not touching items in a museum display. Social stories can also help to prepare them for situations they may find difficult over the course of the day, such as being surrounded by lots of other people.

If you are visiting a particular venue, contact them to:

- Explain the needs of the child and ask how they can support the child. Make sure the destination knows if the child has any sensory issues or particular dietary requirements.
- Ask if they have a quiet area for the child to take a break, if needed.
- Arrange a pre-visit for yourself so you can identify any areas that might trigger problems for the child, and plan accordingly.
- Ask if you can bring the child for a pre-visit at a quiet time of the week.

A week or two before you go, talk to the child about when the visit will take place. Make a countdown calendar so the child can mark off how many days are left until they go.

Think about particular times during the outing that the child might find difficult. For example, they might struggle at lunchtime free play because they don't know what to do with themselves. If so, remember to take books, games, or tablet devices to keep the child occupied. Sit down and plan through the day step by step, so you can tailor your strategies and pack appropriate resources for the child.

On the day, if you're travelling by coach board quickly, keeping goodbyes to parents brief, so the child doesn't have time to feel more anxious. On board, give the child games or activities that relate to their particular interests, favourite music or a portable DVD player if it helps (being aware of travel sickness!).

Some destinations offer tailor-made programmes for children with a spectrum of special educational needs and disability, employ SEND qualified staff, and have full accessibility for children with severe physical needs: SEN Outdoor Education, Plan My School Trip - https://www.planmyschooltrip.co.uk/special-educational-needs.php

Story time

When a child has attention difficulties, story times can be a challenge, but there are ways to make sure story times are engaging for everyone.

Share sensory stories (those involving smell, sound, sight, and touch). Books for babies are often tactile, visual and auditory – think of the 'That's not my…' Usborne series and all those noise and sound button books.

Ordinary children's picture books can be made into sensory experiences using props to convey the story's sensations. You can even write your own simple stories based on children's interests and experiences, presenting them using sensory props.

Find out more about multi-sensory stories here: https://www.essexlocaloffer.org.uk/wp-content/uploads/2017/01/Sensational-Stories-MASTER.pdf

When sharing non-sensory stories think of ways children can actively participate. They could point to pictures, turn pages, answer questions, or hold up items related

Chapter 7: Removing barriers to learning

to events as the story unfolds. Give children puppets and props so they can act out the story as they listen, or ask them to listen out for specific things in the story.

Here are some more tips:

- Share big books with large print, pointing to the words as you read.
- As you read, put on the voices of different characters to hold children's interest.
- Share stories in both large and small groups to suit all children.
- Make sure the book corner is comfortable and free from elements that could distract a child with a particular need.
- Promote independence in the book corner by including:
  - Recorded stories with colour-coded 'play' and 'stop' buttons.
  - Braille books and books that use sign language in the book corner if needed.
  - A visual routine chart which shows the child, step by step, what to do, eg. choose a book from the box, sit on a cushion, open the book, look at the book quietly.

- For a child who has trouble turning the pages of the book, place pieces of sticky foam between the pages so there's more room for their fingers.

Tidy up time

- Warn all children a few minutes before tidy up time.
- Expect all children to tidy up. Place little baskets on wheelchairs or give children with crutches waist bags so they can collect and move resources from place to place.
- Model appropriate behaviour by tidying up with the children.
- Label boxes with pictures so children know where everything goes.
- Help a child with sight difficulties by clearly outlining shelf areas with contrasting colours or different textures.

Transition times

Use cues that all children understand to indicate transition times, eg. a bell to signal lunchtime, a 'tidy up time' song, a picture cues for snack time etc. To help a child who has difficulties managing transitions you could:

- Decide whether lining all the children up together is the best way for the child to move between areas.
- Think about moving a small group at a time.
- Show how you would like everyone to line up by asking one child to demonstrate.
- Use lining up times as opportunities to forward learning and keep everyone busy by, for example, practising numbers or positional language, or listening for sounds.
- Make sure the time children are expected to stand still for is brief.
- Motivate the child with particular difficulties by giving them a specific job to do, like holding the door open.
- Provide the child with a coat peg that is on the end of a row so it's easier to find.

All these actions will help children during the crucial transition period between home and setting, or between setting and school.

Child Protection and SEND

Often the words 'safeguarding' and 'child protection' are used interchangeably. Safeguarding covers everything an educational institution does to keep children safe. This includes following health and safety procedures like maintaining equipment and buildings, educating children about e-safety, keeping records of attendance, ensuring the curriculum is inclusive, and child protection.

This chapter exclusively covers child protection. Child protection refers to the activities undertaken by schools and settings to protect children from suffering harm.

Under Section 31 (9) of the Children Act 1989, harm is defined as:

- Ill-treatment which includes emotional abuse, neglect and sexual abuse.
- Damage to the physical or mental health of a child, which includes the psychological damage that arises from seeing or hearing another person suffering harm.
- Impairing a child's emotional, behavioural, intellectual or emotional development.

The child protection procedures put in place to protect children with special educational needs and disability (SEND) from harm are the same as for all children. However, children with SEND are statistically more vulnerable to abuse and so additional measures need to be put in place.

'Statistically, children with special educational needs and/or disabilities (SEND) are most vulnerable to abuse... Children who have difficulty with expressive language may be particularly vulnerable to abuse so practitioners will be alert to changes in behaviour and other possible signs of abuse.'
Safeguarding disabled children: Practice guidance, 2009

Here's the most current government guidance on child protection (at the time this book was published):

- Keeping children safe in education: statutory guidance for schools and colleges (note: 'schools' also includes 'maintained nursery schools').
- Working Together to Safeguard Children 2018.

- What to do if you're worried a child is being abused: advice for practitioners.

For children with special educational needs and disability you need to read Safeguarding disabled children: Practice guidance, 2009. All links are listed under 'Government guidance' in Chapter 10.

Which legislation covers child protection?

There isn't just one piece of legislation that covers child protection because the law is continually changing. The Children Act 1989 provides the framework for child protection, and is supplemented by the Children Act 2004.

The Children Act 2004 is solely about safeguarding. It came about as a direct response to the Victoria Climbié inquiry. Victoria, an eight year old from Abidjan who had moved to London with her aunt, was starved, beaten, tortured and neglected over many months. The inquiry found that her death might have been prevented if there had not been gaps in her care due to a number of inter-agency failings, including a lack of communication. The Children Act 2004 was put in place to ensure such failings will never happen again. The Act supports professionals to work together and share information, ensures clear accountability of children's services, establishes Local Safeguarding Children's Boards (LSCBs), and ensures a voice for children and young people.

The Children and Social Work Act 2017 amends the Children Act 2004 by replacing LSCBs with 'local safeguarding partners'. The three partners (local authorities, the police, and the health service) now have equal and joint responsibility for local safeguarding instead of operating through an independent LSCB chair. The three partners must work with other relevant agencies – which includes schools and early years providers – to ensure children are safe and protected. Nadhim Zahawi, who was Children's Minister until 2019, said that the change will result in a stronger safeguarding system which places greater accountability on key professionals and a more collaborative approach to decision making. The changes are continually under review. At the time of publication local authorities are in a state of transition. See the government document,

Working Together: transitional guidance, July 2018 (listed under 'Government guidance', see page 117).

It is important to understand that the General Data Protection Regulation 2018 (GDPR) does not prevent staff from sharing information with relevant agencies if that information helps to protect a child. The GDPR is about protecting people's personal information from inappropriate sharing. It is not a barrier to child protection!

Who is responsible for child protection?

The Children and Social Work Act 2017 states that local authorities, the police, and the health service are ultimately responsible for child protection. Those three partners must work together with other relevant agencies – which includes schools and early years settings – to identify and support children who are at risk of harm.

The government guidance, Working Together to Safeguard Children 2018, makes it clear that:

- Everyone who works with children has a responsibility to keep them safe.
- Everyone who comes into contact with children and families has a role to play in identifying concerns and sharing information.

Who is in charge of child protection in the setting?

All settings must have a Designated Person in charge of child protection (DP). This is normally the most senior member of staff. The DP must:

- Refer cases of suspected child abuse to the local authority's social care.
- Be alert to the specific vulnerabilities of children with special educational needs and disability.
- Refer child abuse cases where a crime has been committed to the police.
- Where radicalisation is suspected, refer cases to the Channel programme. See HM Government's Channel guidance - the link is under 'Government guidance', see page 117.

- Undertake child protection training which must be updated at least every three years.
- Undertake Prevent awareness training.
- Refresh their child protection knowledge constantly by attending local authority safeguarding meetings, reading bulletins etc.
- Keep detailed, accurate child protection records.
- Ensure that staff are trained in child protection so that they can identify signs of abuse and know how to log and report concerns.

Review the setting's child protection policy at least annually, and ensure that if there are any changes staff and parents are told.

What are the types of abuse?

Emotional

This is treatment that harms a child's emotional development. The child might be made to feel worthless and unloved. They may be ridiculed or silenced from sharing their views. Emotional abuse can also be in the form of overprotection, whereby the child is denied social or learning experiences. It might be treating a child as an adult by exposing them to inappropriate behaviour or treatment. It includes any behaviour that causes a child to feel frightened and insecure.

Neglect

The failure to meet the child's physical and/or emotional needs. This can be failure to provide adequate clothing, food and shelter. It is the failure to meet the child's needs in any way, including by withholding medical treatment or exposing them to danger through poor supervision.

Physical

Any act that physically harms a child. A child can be physically harmed if a carer fabricates the symptoms of an illness in a child or deliberately causes illness. Physical abuse includes female genital mutilation (FGM). Female genital mutilation - where the female genitals are cut or changed without medical reason - is carried out on females of all ages – see 'References' in Chapter 10 for the NHS website.

Radicalisation

Under the Counter-Terrorism and Security Act 2015, professionals have a duty to prevent children from being 'radicalised' (drawn into terrorism). This is called the 'Prevent Duty'. See the government document, The Prevent duty, 2015, listed under 'References: Government guidance', see page 118.

Sexual

Forcing or enticing a child to take part in sexual activities. It is not only adult males who perpetrate sexual abuse, but also females and other children.

Why are children with SEND particularly vulnerable to abuse?

Any child can be a victim of abuse, but professionals who work with children who have SEND need to be aware that these children are particularly vulnerable.

Here are some reasons why children with SEND are more vulnerable to abuse:

- They are more likely to have fewer outside social contacts than non-disabled children, which makes it more difficult for them to access someone they can trust to listen to them.
- They depend upon others for practical assistance, including intimate personal care which increases their exposure to risk.
- They have impaired ability to resist abuse.
- They might have a speech, language and communication impairment, which makes it harder for them to tell others what is happening to them.
- They are more vulnerable to bullying and intimidation (see 'Bullying' further below).
- Most children with SEND are likely to spend some time away from their families in residential care and health settings. As they are dependent upon residential and hospital staff to care for their physical needs this puts them at increased risk. Abusive behaviour could be force feeding, rough handling, excessive restraint, extreme discipline such as depriving the child of food or water, misuse of medication, or undignified intimate care.

'Disabled children are more likely to experience abuse than non-disabled children. Children living away from home are particularly vulnerable.'
Disabled Children and Young People and those with Complex Health Needs, Department for Education and Skills, 2004

The most vulnerable children of all are those with special educational needs and disability who are also 'looked after' (in care).

What are the signs that abuse is taking place?

Signs of abuse are covered in the Basic Child Protection Training that all early years practitioners undertake. To refresh your knowledge read the NSPCC's Definitions and Signs of Child Abuse (see 'References' in Chapter 10).

Practitioners working with children who have SEND, particularly those who have communication challenges, need to be particularly alert for behavioural changes that might indicate abuse is taking place. Specialist

training on protecting children with SEND from abuse is available (see 'Training' on p.92).

Bullying

According to the Institute of Education, children with special educational needs are twice as likely to be bullied than other children.[12]

To prevent bullying, settings need:

- Rigorous anti-bullying and behaviour policies that are shared with and upheld by all staff and parents.
- Zero tolerance to bullying with firm, disciplinary procedures that are shared with parents.
- Staff training on preventing bullying.
- An inclusive, caring ethos, which can be achieved by:
  - Educating all children about special educational needs and disability to raise awareness and promote empathy.
  - Fostering inclusive language and attitudes in the setting. See Chapter 7 for ideas about how to put this into practice.

- Support for children with SEND to help them to make and maintain friendships.
- To teach children anti-bullying strategies which are appropriate for their age and developmental stage.
- Keen adult supervision, especially during free play when bullying is more likely to occur.

10 steps to help reduce children with SEND's vulnerability to abuse

1. Encourage children to communicate their feelings and opinions about their treatment and care. The UN Convention on the Rights of the Child says that every child has a right to express their opinions on decisions and actions that affect them and to have their views taken seriously. The Children Act 1989 and the Children Act 2004 make it clear that professionals must listen to and value children's wishes regarding their own care.

2. When children have difficulty communicating, seek specialist advice. There are a range of

communication systems including British Sign Language[13] and Makaton[14]. It is vital that children can communicate their needs, wishes and worries to those around them and be understood, listened to and valued. On page 73-77 of Safeguarding Disabled Children: Practice guidance, you will find a list of websites containing resources to support communication.

3. Teach children with SEND how to raise concerns and give them access to a range of adults who can help them.

4. Do everything possible to prevent bullying, and to deal effectively with instances of bullying if they occur (see 'Bullying' above).

5. Incorporate SEND into all staff's basic child protection training. (See 'Training' on p.92).

6. Staff must be trained on good practice in handling challenging behaviour, working with children of the opposite sex, intimate care, and consent to treatment. They must be able to identify the signs of abuse, and know how to record and report concerns appropriately.

7. The setting's child protection policy should make it clear that the same procedures are followed, regardless of whether a child has SEND or not. The policy should highlight the additional barriers that adults may face in identifying abuse in children with SEND and how these barriers are addressed. (See 'Your setting's child protection policy and SEND' on p.89).

8. Children should be safeguarded and staff protected with a clear intimate care policy. The policy should state that children are treated with sensitivity and respect, and that the parent is consulted about the intimate care of their child.

9. Children should receive appropriate health, personal, social and sex education so they can more easily identify harmful treatment, particularly regarding what is suitable and inappropriate physical contact.

10. Establish a relationship with families that encourages a culture of openness and information sharing.

What procedures must you follow if you suspect abuse is taking place?

- If you believe the child is in immediate danger call the police on 999.
- If the danger is not immediate then you must speak to your setting's designated person in charge of child protection (DP) and follow your setting's child protection procedures. The procedures will be in line with your local authority's child protection and safeguarding procedures. More information can be found on your local authority's website.
- Childminders can seek advice from their local childminding support and development officer (CSDO).
- You can also contact the NSPCC helpline on 0808 800 5000 for expert advice from trained professionals.
- It is compulsory for all professionals in contact with children to report known cases of female genital mutilation (FGM). If the danger is immediate call the police. If not, call the FGM helpline on 0800 028 3550 or email fgmhelp@nspcc.org.uk

Read the government's non-statutory advice, What to do if you're worried a child is being abused: advice for practitioners. The link is listed under 'References' in Chapter 10.

Your setting's child protection policy and SEND

Most children with special educational needs attend mainstream settings rather than special schools, so it is important that specific reference is made to SEND in your child protection policy.

Your setting's policy should be clear that:

- All practitioners understand that high self-esteem, supportive friends, and strong lines of communication with a trusted adult help to protect all children from abuse.
- All forms of abuse (including peer-on-peer) are unacceptable.
- Practitioners know that statistically, children with SEND are more vulnerable to abuse.

- Practitioners who look after children with SEND are particularly alert to signs of abuse.

The policy could say how your setting supports practitioners to raise children's self-esteem and to manage challenging behaviour in partnership with parents. It might explain that children are taught personal safety skills appropriate to their ability, so that they can distinguish abusive behaviour from non-abusive behaviour and they know who to tell if they are worried.

The policy could state that children with communication difficulties are particularly vulnerable to abuse and so practitioners are trained to recognise behavioural changes as potential indicators. It could explain that, when needed, the setting provides additional training for practitioners to use communication systems, such as Makaton[15] or Picture Exchange Communication System (PECS),[16] to support children's communication.

The policy should cross-reference your setting's anti-bullying policy, behaviour policy, and intimate care policy.

The very best way to understand how your setting's child protection policy could have a strong special educational needs and disability element, is to look at child protection policies on your local special school websites.

Training

Your local authority will offer a range of mandatory and non-mandatory training courses on safeguarding and child protection. These will include:

- Designated Person for Child Protection courses and refresher courses.
- Basic Child Protection Training.

The above courses cover some of the particular challenges of protecting children with SEND. However, it is beneficial – especially if you are the designated person (DP) – to supplement your learning with more specific courses, such as:

- High Speed Training's Safeguarding Children with Disabilities Training Course: https://www.highspeedtraining.co.uk/safeguarding-people/safeguarding-children-with-disabilities-training-course.aspx
- The Children Society's Communicating with Disabled Children and Young People: https://www.childrenssociety.org.uk/sites/default/files/tcs/communicating_with_disabled_children__young_people.pdf

Check your local authority's website for training courses too.

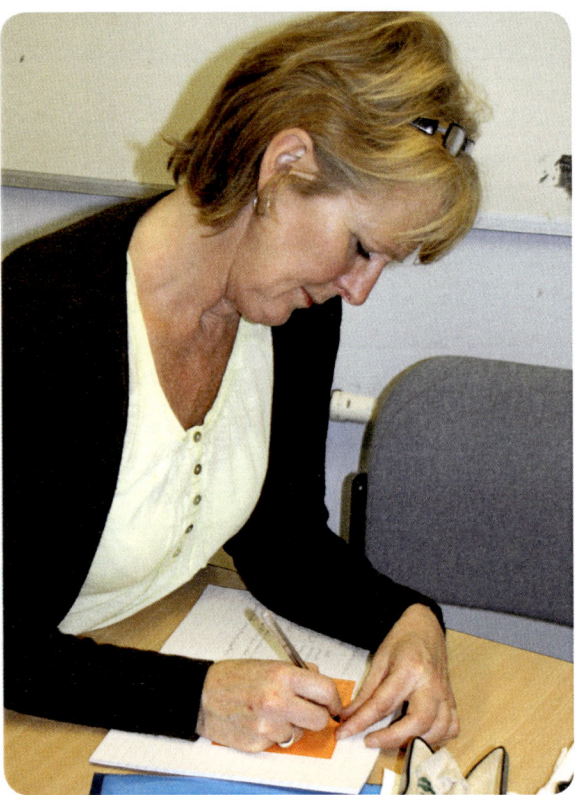

Funding and Benefits

Children from lower income families are more than twice as likely to be identified as having special educational needs and disabilities (SEND) and yet are less likely to receive the support they need, according to a study carried out by the Joseph Rowntree Foundation.[17]

Families find it difficult to identify their entitlements because, although local authority 'local offer' websites should provide the solution, in practice, the clarity of communication varies across the country.

The main barrier is the complexity of the system, so it is helpful to be able to signpost parents towards funding and benefits available for their children.

The child and their family

In this chapter, as well as providing an overview of funding and possible benefits for families, we also summarise the funding that your setting may be able to access themselves directly.

Although this is your setting manager or proprietor's area of responsibility, we think it would be useful for you to have some background knowledge of how the system works. Receiving the right financial and practical support both at home and in the setting helps children with SEND to thrive.

Working out the child's entitlement

When it is first thought a child has SEND, the local authority's Early Support team will carry out an Early Help Assessment (EHA) – see Chapter 3. However, if it is thought the child needs more support than can be offered through an EHA, then a 'child in need assessment' or 'social care assessment' will take place.

Local authorities have a duty under the Children Act 1989 to assess all children 'in need' – see Chapter 2.

If a local authority refuses to carry out an assessment on the grounds that a child's disabilities are not severe enough, parents can ask for a written explanation.

Chapter 9: Funding and Benefits

It is important for parents to know that their child could still be defined as a 'child in need' even if they don't meet the legal definition of 'disabled'. The government's statutory guidance, Working Together to Safeguard Children: 2018, explains child in need assessments in full.

Both the views of the parents and the child are central to any decisions the local authority makes regarding their care. This is set out in the Children and Families Act 2014, Section 19.

Before a child in need assessment takes place, it's a good idea for families to familiarise themselves with the documents the local authority has published on their website regarding the social care provision for disabled children (if they aren't available on the website you can ring the local authority and ask for them). The threshold documents are particularly useful in helping families to understand what their entitlement is. As an example, here is Cambridgeshire County Council's page. The threshold document here is called 'eligibility criteria document': https://www.cambridgeshire.gov.uk/residents/children-and-families/children-s-social-care/disability-social-care-0-25/

Parents of disabled children also have a right to have their own needs assessed – this is called a Parent Carer's Needs Assessment (PCNA). This takes place as part of the child in need assessment.

What's the connection between a child in need assessment and an EHC needs assessment?

If a child meets the legal definition of 'child in need' and also has a learning disability as defined in the Children and Families Act 2014, they will be entitled to both types of assessment. It is likely that the local authority will carry out both assessments at the same time, if possible, in order to mimimise disruption to the family.

What particular needs are assessed in a child in need assessment?

The child in need assessment will be carried out by a social worker employed by the local authority. The purpose of the assessment is to discover the child's and family's specific needs and which social care support services will address those needs. The assessment will take into account:

- The child's disabilities and needs.
- The parents' needs – the social worker will simultaneously carry out a Parent Carer Needs Assessment (PCNA)
- How the whole family's life is impacted by the child's needs.
- The suitability of the home environment for meeting the child's needs.

The purpose of the assessment is to ensure that support is put in place to promote the child's wellbeing and the wellbeing of their family. 'Wellbeing' includes:

- Physical, emotional and social health.
- Protection from abuse.
- Having control over day-to-day life.
- Being able to participate in education, work or recreation so they contribute to society.
- Economic wellbeing.
- Happy and healthy personal relationships.

It is important that the whole family receives help so they do not sink under the pressures of caring for a child with

SEND. The first rule of caring is to care for the carer! A major consideration in the assessment is how siblings' lives are affected and what provision can be put in place so that they enjoy the same quality of life as most other children their age.

What support might be received following an assessment?

The Chronically Sick and Disabled Person's Act 1970 states what local authorities must provide by law. The Act can be found online. In summary, it includes:

- Short break services for both the child and their family (See 'Short breaks' in Chapter 2)
- Holiday play schemes.
- Home help with day-to-day tasks, such as cooking and laundry.
- Aids and adaptations to the home.
- Financial assistance. See 'Personal budgets and direct payments' in Chapter 2.

The social worker will set out the support that will be provided for the child and family in a care plan (sometimes called a 'plan of action' or 'support plan').

Local authorities don't usually charge parents for the services they provide but they are allowed to do so under the law. As budgets become tighter the likelihood that parents will have to meet some costs increases. However, local authorities cannot charge parents more than they can reasonably afford as set out under Section 29 (3) of the Children Act 1989.

What other funding and benefits can a family receive?

This is a list of the funding children with SEND and their families may be entitled to receive.

Disability Living Allowance (DLA)

DLA is the main financial benefit for disabled children. It isn't means tested or taxable and it can make a huge difference to a family's income.

DLA is divided into two parts – Mobility and Care – which are both covered on the same application form. DLA is paid at three rates:

- Low rate. When a child needs additional care for more than an hour a day.
- Middle rate. If the child needs care all day or at night.
- High rate. If the child needs care all day and all night.

Qualifying for DLA can mean a family is eligible for other benefits or an increase in existing benefits too. It is wise for parents to alert the authorities that their child is in receipt of DLA in order to receive these additional benefits.

1. Free early years education
   Some children with DLA qualify for 15 hours free education when they are two years old. Other children do not qualify until they are three.

2. Carer's Allowance (CA)
   If a child receives middle or high rate DLA the parent may qualify for CA. They must be caring for the child for at least 35 hours a week. CA can negatively affect other benefits such as Income Support, but in most cases it's still worth claiming.

3. Income Support (IS)
   Families who receive IS will receive extra money if their child receives DLA. This is called the Disabled

Chapter 9: Funding and Benefits

Child Premium which is higher with higher rate DLA. Parents will need to let the Job Centre who processes their Income Support know.

4. Housing Benefit and Council Tax
   DLA can lead to extra benefit. Parents need to inform the local council that their child receives DLA.

5. Universal Credit
   This is positively affected by DLA – see below.

6. Benefit Cap Exemption
   Families with children who receive DLA are exempt from the 'benefit cap', which restricts the amount of benefit payments out of work parents can receive.

7. Parking
   Blue badges are awarded to drivers with children on high rate DLA, but there are also other qualifications too, including children who cannot undertake a journey without considerable mental distress. It is worthwhile parents checking eligibility rules: https://www.gov.uk/apply-blue-badge

   People with hidden disabilities such as anxiety or autism can also apply for a blue badge: https://www.gov.uk/government/news/people-with-hidden-disabilities-can-access-blue-badges-for-the-first-time-from-today

8. Road tax
   Those who have a child with high rate DLA are exempt from paying Vehicle Excise Duty.

9. Mobility
   Families with children who are on high rate DLA can lease a car through the Motability Scheme: https://www.motability.co.uk/

10. Free bus travel
    Under-fives usually travel free of charge anyway, but some local authorities also provide free travel for a named carer.

For more about DLA, see Contact's two factsheets: https://contact.org.uk/media/1545694/claiming_dla_for_children.pdf https://contact.org.uk/media/1188031/dla_for_children_with_autism_and_learning_difficulties.pdf

Universal Credit

This is a benefit administered by the Department for Work and Pensions (DWP) and paid to people over the age of sixteen. The reason we've included it here is because if a parent cares for a severely disabled child for 35 or more hours a week they are eligible for Universal Credit under the 'Carer element'.

An additional amount is also payable for each child who is on Disability Living Allowance (DLA) or who is registered sight impaired.

For more, see Contact's factsheet 'Universal Credit: the essentials': https://contact.org.uk/media/1524385/universal_credit_the_essentials.pdf

Personal health budget

Children who qualify for the NHS's Continuing Healthcare Package are entitled to a personal health budget. These are children with severe and complex health needs. For more information read 'National Framework for Children and Young People's Continuing Care': https://assets.publishing.service.gov.uk/government/uploads/system/uploads/attachment_data/file/499611/children_s_continuing_care_Fe_16.pdf

Personal health budgets give parents the flexibility to plan their child's own health care by paying directly for the services and equipment that they believe best meets the child's needs.

To discover if their child is eligible, parents need to visit their local Clinical Commissioning Group website. Find this by typing the local authority name followed by 'personal health budget' into a search engine, eg. 'Manchester personal health budget'.

Integrated personal budget

This is the term used when a child's personal health budget and personal budget (see 'Personal budgets and direct payments' under the Children and Families Act 2014 in Chapter 2) are combined.

Disabled Facilities Grant (DFG)

This local authority grant is to pay for the home adaptations necessary for the disabled person to live as independent a life as possible. Changes might include door widening, installing ramps or lifts, building a new bedroom or providing access to the garden.

The grant is payable by the local council following an assessment by a social worker and an occupational therapist. More information can be found here: https://www.gov.uk/disabled-facilities-grants

Transport costs

Children under the age of five are not automatically entitled to funded transport to and from the setting. However, the Education Act 1996 (Section 509A) gives local authorities the discretion to provide transport for children in early years settings and they are not allowed to 'fetter their discretion'. That means they cannot refuse to provide transport just because it's not their duty under the law. If a child's particular disability means they cannot attend the setting without transport from the local authority, then parents can appeal a refusal.

Family Fund

Family Fund is a UK charity that provides grants for families raising a disabled or seriously ill child. Parents can apply for grants for all sorts of items – washing machines, sensory equipment, family breaks, clothes, tablets and more: https://www.familyfund.org.uk/

Other grants

There are all sorts of other grants families can receive covering everything from fulfilling children's dreams and wishes, to providing funds for children with specific conditions.

Parents can find out more from:

Turn2Us: https://www.turn2us.org.uk/
Disability Grants: https://www.disability-grants.org/grants-for-children.html

Parents could also contact their child's relevant charity, eg. Down's Syndrome Association or the National Autistic Society, to find out whether they offer grants.

Further support for parents

For personalised financial advice, parents could contact:

The Money Advice Service: https://www.moneyadviceservice.org.uk/en
Citizens Advice: https://www.citizensadvice.org.uk/
Contact: for families with disabled children: https://contact.org.uk/

Funding in the setting

What local authority funding is allocated to the setting?

Local authority funding for two, three and four year olds comes from the Early Years Block of the Dedicated Schools Grant (DSG). As well as providing free childcare entitlement to three and four year olds, local authorities use the Early Years Block to fund:

- Early years entitlement for eligible two year olds.
- Supplementary funding for Maintained Nursery Schools (MNS).
- Early Years Pupil Premium (EYPP).
- Disability Access Fund (DAF).
- Special Educational Needs Inclusion Fund (SENIF) for three and four year olds.
- High needs funding.

The Early Years National Funding Formula (EYNFF) sets out the hourly funding rates that local authorities are paid by central government to deliver these entitlements. Hourly rates vary between areas. To find out about

Chapter 9: Funding and Benefits

funding rates in your area look at, 'Early years national funding formula: funding rates and guidance' (See link under Government guidance in Chapter 10).

Early Years Pupil Premium (EYPP)

The EYPP is funding to help settings support disadvantaged three and four year olds. It is not specifically SEND money, but if a child with SEND happens to be eligible for EYPP then it can be used to address those needs.

To qualify for EYPP, children must be eligible for at least 15 hours early years entitlement and meet one or more of the following criteria:

- That their family receives support with one of the following entitlements:
  Income Support, Jobseeker's Allowance, income-related Employment and Support Allowance, support under the Immigration and Asylum Act 1999 (part VI), the guaranteed element of State Pension Credit, Working Tax Credit, Universal Credit.
- They are looked after by the local authority.
- They are under an adoption order, a special guardianship order, or a child arrangements order.

For SEND, the EYPP could be spent in any number of ways, such as:

- Non-contact time to allow for planning and resourcing targeted activities.
- Additional staff for 1:1 work, such as speech and language.
- Play sacks to take home in order to encourage high quality interactions.
- Funding transport, if needed, for the child to attend the setting.

Disability Access Fund (DAF)

The Equality Act 2010 requires settings to make 'reasonable adjustments' to include disabled children.

The DAF provides funds for settings to make reasonable adjustments for three and four year olds. Settings receive £615 per year for each eligible child. A reasonable adjustment could, amongst other things, be purchasing specialist equipment, adapting the physical environment or providing one to one support. See 'Reasonable adjustments' under the Equality Act 2010 in Chapter 2 for more.

Three and four year olds qualify for DAF if they:

- Are eligible for at least 15 hours free childcare, whether or not they take up their whole allotment.
- Receive Disability Living Allowance (DLA).

Four year olds in school Reception classes are not eligible for DAF.

Special Educational Needs Inclusion Fund (SENIF)

Local authorities must have a SENIF for all three and four year olds with SEND who are eligible for free childcare hours (whether or not they take up their whole entitlement). This fund supports local authorities to meet their duties under the Children and Families Act 2014.

The SENIF is for children with emerging or lower levels of SEND – those who are listed on the setting's SEN Register. Children with EHCPs or complex and severe needs receive 'high needs funding' instead (see below).

The value of the SENIF varies between local authorities who take into account the need in their local area. Local authorities 'must consult with early years providers to set the value of their local SEN inclusion fund' and they must 'consult with early years providers, parents and SEN specialists on how the SEN inclusion fund will be allocated, as part of the preparation and review of their 'Local Offer'' ('Early years entitlements: local authority funding of providers: operational guide 2019-2020', Sections 55 and 57).

Local authorities have to pass on most of the SENIF to early years providers 'in the form of 'top up grants' on a case-by-case basis' (Early years entitlements: local authority funding of providers: operational guide 2019-2020', Section 58). They can also use the SENIF to pay for specialist SEND support services in their area.

Under the local offer 'local authorities should publish details on how they are using their SEN inclusion fund to support their early years SEN cohort' (Early years entitlements: local authority funding of providers: operational guide 2019-2020, Section 57).

In the setting, SENIF money can be used to fund any provision that enables the child to access the EYFS curriculum. It could pay for additional staff and resources, training to help staff to meet a child's specific special needs and disabilities, or specialist equipment.

High Needs Funding

Children who are receiving 15 or 30 hours free childcare and who have complex and severe needs (whether or not they have an EHCP) are eligible for funding under the 'high needs' block of the Dedicated Schools Grant (DSG).

This extra funding is available when their needs are so significant that the SENIF and DAF don't allow enough money for the local authority to fulfil their duties under the Children and Families Act 2014.

The term 'severe and complex needs' describes children with multiple barriers to learning such as cognition, communication, physical and sensory. For example, children with Autism Spectrum Disorder (ASD) may be described as such if they have a combination of difficulties.

Are there any grants the setting can apply for?

Yes, but there is plenty of competition. It is still worth applying to these organisations if you believe you can make a strong application:

Early Years Alliance - Small Grants, Big Difference
https://www.eyalliance.org.uk/small-grants-big-difference

Funding Grants – Early Years Foundation Funding
https://funding-grants.co.uk/education-grants/early-years-foundation-stage

You must be able to explain how the grant will be spent and clearly communicate the definite long-term benefits to the child or children in your setting. The Early Years Alliance prioritise applications benefiting children from disadvantaged backgrounds and those with SEND.

Resources and training

This Chapter is made of a collection of resources that have been referred to throughout this book.

Their aim is to help early years practitioners, or all those who care for children with SEND whether within the setting or at home, with useful and practical information in support of the needs of the child or their day to day caring activities.

These resources will range from:
- Photocopiable activities.
- Sheets and forms that will help both the SENCO and the parent to assess, plan and review the next steps for their children.
- Templates to record the information.
- Guidance and links to websites of organisations providing support, through to further specialist and professional training for staff and practitioners.

All this material will give additional pointers to legislation and government policy, as well as further references for where to find the information you need on the internet.

At the time of writing, the world had been dramatically impacted by the coronavirus pandemic.

Additional information was therefore added, in support of those who may need clarification on ways in which children who were affected by the pandemic and their families, can be further supported.

All references have been updated with current legislation and website links checked at the time of publishing. However, please check the relevant sites regularly for any change in policies and documentation, as these are likely to change from time to time, or to find out about any more types of assistance that may be available to children and parents, or the setting themselves.

It is hoped that this book will be a valuable guide during your journey working with children with SEND, their families, and beyond.

All About Me

My name:	Today's date:

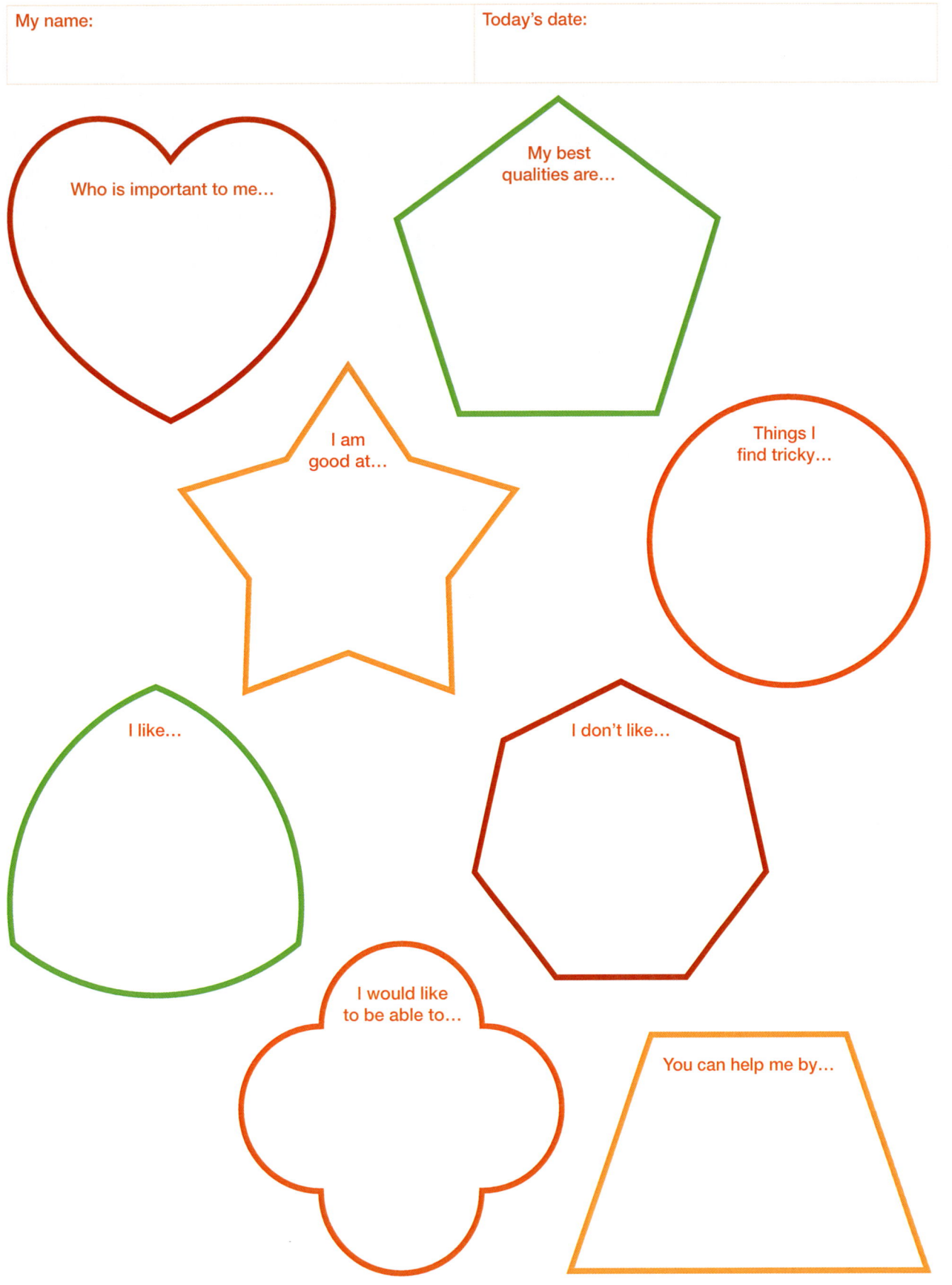

Who is important to me…

My best qualities are…

I am good at…

Things I find tricky…

I like…

I don't like…

I would like to be able to…

You can help me by…

Assessment tools and intervention programmes

Area of need	Possible assessment tools	Intervention programmes
Physical	Early Years Assessment: Physical Development – Moving and Handling by Trudi Fitzhenry and Karen Murphy: https://www.bloomsbury.com/uk/early-years-assessment-physical-development-9781472954565/ Gross Motor Development Chart: https://childdevelopment.com.au/resources/child-development-charts/gross-motor-developmental-chart/	Encouraging Early Sports Skills by Sandy and Jake Green Planning for Learning Through Games by Rachel Sparks Linfield https://www.practicalpreschoolbooks.com/physical-development Sensory Circuits: A sensory motor skills programme for children by Jane Horwood The Little Book of Scissor Skills by Sharon Drew https://www.bloomsbury.com/uk/the-little-book-of-scissor-skills-9781906029333/ Physical Development – Moving and Handling by Trudi Fitzhenry and Karen Murphy https://www.bloomsbury.com/uk/education/early-years/physical-development/
Cognition	Bayley III Screening Test https://www.pearsonclinical.co.uk/Psychology/ChildCognitionNeuropsychologyandLanguage/ChildGeneralAbilities/Bayley-IIIScreeningTest/Bayley-IIIScreeningTest.aspx Mullen Scales of Early Learning https://www.pearsonclinical.co.uk/Psychology/ChildCognitionNeuropsychologyandLanguage/ChildGeneralAbilities/mullen/mullen-scales-of-early-learning.aspx	See 'Communication and Language'.
Communication and language	The Renfrew Language Scales Assessment: http://soundingboard.earfoundation.org.uk/resources/?cat=6&sub_cat_id=19&page=113 The British Picture Vocabulary Scale (BPVS): https://www.gl-assessment.co.uk/products/british-picture-vocabulary-scale-bpvs3/ Afasic: http://www.afasic.org.uk/resources/ The Communication Trust: https://www.thecommunicationtrust.org.uk/resources/resources/resources-for-practitioners/progression-tools-primary/ I Can: https://ican.org.uk/i-cans-talking-point/ Test of Abstract Language Comprehension (TALC2): https://elklantraining.worldsecuresystems.com/ Derbyshire Language Scheme: https://www.derbyshire-language-scheme.co.uk Wellcom: https://www.gl-assessment.co.uk/wellcomm	Early Talk "For early years practitioners working with groups of 3 to 4 year olds with delayed language. The programme aims to accelerate children's progress in language and communication by an average of six months, after a nine week intervention." https://ican.org.uk/training-licensing/i-can-programmes/ Chatty Bats "Chatty Bats is an impactful language development programme for children age 3 to 5 years old." https://www.lingospeech.co.uk/resources/ Chatterboxes "Chatterboxes are boxes of games and activities to support listening, understanding and talking for 3 to 5 year olds." https://www.lingospeech.co.uk/resources/ Nuffield Early Language Intervention "The Nuffield Early Language Intervention is an evidence-based oral language intervention for children in nursery and Reception." https://www.nuffieldfoundation.org/nuffield-early-language-intervention Attention Autism "Aims to develop natural and spontaneous communication through the use of visually based and highly motivating activities." http://best-practice.middletownautism.com/approaches-of-intervention/attention-autism/

Area of need	Possible assessment tools	Intervention programmes
Literacy	Comprehensive Test of Phonological Processing (CTOPP-2): https://www.pearsonclinical.co.uk/ AlliedHealth/PaediatricAssessments/PhonologicalAwareness/ctopp-2/comprehensive-test-of-phonological-processing-second-edition.aspx York Assessment of Reading Comprehension (YARC): http://www.gl-education.com	Get Ready for Phonics "Get ready for Phonics" is a targeted intervention to support phonological awareness and vocabulary learning. Aimed at children aged 4-6 years." https://www.lingospeech.co.uk/resources/
Maths	Sandwell Early Numeracy Test: http://www.sandwellearlynumeracytest.co.uk	Maths Champions http://www.ndna.org.uk/childcare-training-maths-champions This programme "boosts the confidence and skills" of early years practitioners so they can help children to gain "a stronger foundation in maths from birth upwards". Practitioners will be able to devise their own targeted intervention programmes using the skills they have learnt.
Personal, Social and Emotional	Strengths and Difficulties Questionnaire (SDQ): http://www.sdqinfo.com/ The Boxall Profile: https://www.nurtureuk.org/introducing-nurture/boxall-profile Early Years Assessment: Personal Social and Emotional Development by Trudi Fitzhenry and Karen Murphy: https://www.bloomsbury.com/uk/early-years-assessment-personal-social-and-emotional-development-9781472955050/	Social and Emotional Intervention Kit "An activity programme to support the social and emotional needs of children." https://www.tts-group.co.uk/social-and-emotional-intervention-kit/1011347.html Jigsaw PSHE "Jigsaw PSHE for Early Years, Nurseries and Pre-schools (Ages 3-4) integrates emotional literacy, self-regulation of behaviour, social skills and spiritual development in an input-per-week programme." https://www.jigsawpshe.com/jigsaw-pshe-for-early-years-nurseries-and-pre-schools-f1-eyfs/ Boxhall Nurture Groups "The nurturing approach offers a range of opportunities for children with missing early nurturing experiences, giving them the social and emotional skills to do well at school and with peers, develop their resilience and their capacity to deal more confidently with the trials and tribulations of life, for life." https://www.nurtureuk.org/nurture/what-nurture-group Self-Regulation Interventions and Strategies: Keeping the Body, Mind & Emotions on Task in Children with Autism, ADHD or Sensory Disorders by Teresa Garland, PESI Publishing and Media, 2014.

Additional Support Plan

Child's name:		Date:	Review date:
Targets	Actions to support achievement of targets	Comments (progress, difficulties, any changes made to objectives) Intervention programmes	Next steps
Example Physical: To be able to control pencil marks	Plenty of opportunities to mark make and to use sensory trays/chalks, whiteboard pens etc.	Fred still needs hand over hand support to control mark making tools.	Fred likes to play in the construction area. Introduce clipboards, pencils, chalks and fine paint brushes into the construction area to maximise practice.

Assess, Plan, Do, Review

Child's name:

Date of birth:

Setting name:

Other professionals involved:

Parents/carers' comments (progress, priorities, concerns):

Graduated approach cycle number:

Date cycle started:

Date cycle finished:

Assess
(Assessments from setting and other professionals)

Plan
(What actions need to be taken?)

Do
(How will these actions be delivered and who is responsible?)

Review
(What progress has been made? What happens next?)

Summative assessment (prime areas)

	0-11	16-26	22-36	30-50	40-60
Personal and Social - Making Relationships:	0-11	16-26	22-36	30-50	40-60
Personal and Social – Self-confidence:	0-11	16-26	22-36	30-50	40-60
Personal and Social – Feelings and Behaviour:	0-11	16-26	22-36	30-50	40-60
Communication and Language - Attention:	0-11	16-26	22-36	30-50	40-60
Communication and Language – Understanding:	0-11	16-26	22-36	30-50	40-60
Communication and Language – Speaking:	0-11	16-26	22-36	30-50	40-60
Physical Development – Moving and Handling:	0-11	16-26	22-36	30-50	40-60
Physical Development – Health and Self-care:	0-11	16-26	22-36	30-50	40-60

Signed by setting:

Signed by parents/carers:

Do

Child's Name:	Practitioner:		Date:
Activity:		Objective:	
What happened?		Outcome	Next Steps

Initial record of concern

Setting:	Date:
Child's name:	
Date of birth:	Number of sessions to date:

Does the child attend another setting?	What is the name of the setting?	How many days/hours does the child attend every week?

Home language:
Medical information:
Specialist services involved to date: *(health, education, social services)*
What are the child's interests?
What are the child's strengths?
What are the areas for concern? Give reasons and examples: *(social and emotional, communication and language, physical, sensory, independence, behaviour, cognition)*
Provide any background information and outline your discussion with parents/carers:
Have you used any specialist assessment tools to diagnose need? What were the results?
What are the next steps? *(placement on SEN register? Further assessment? Specialist support? New approaches to try in the setting?)*
Date of next review:

Parents/carers signature:	Date:
SENCO signature:	

Record of Meeting

Child's Name:	Date:

People present:

Reason for meeting:

What was discussed:

Agreed actions (including who will implement actions):

SENCO signature:

SEND: Early Years Transition

Date:	
Child's name:	Date of birth:
Current setting:	New setting/school:
SEN Support? Yes/no	EHCP? Yes/no

Summative assessment (prime areas)					Areas for development: (eg. communication and language)
Personal and Social - Making Relationships:					
0-11	16-26	22-36	30-50	40-60	
Personal and Social – Self-confidence:					
0-11	16-26	22-36	30-50	40-60	
Personal and Social – Feelings and Behaviour:					
0-11	16-26	22-36	30-50	40-60	
Communication and Language - Attention:					
0-11	16-26	22-36	30-50	40-60	
Communication and Language – Understanding:					
0-11	16-26	22-36	30-50	40-60	
Communication and Language – Speaking:					
0-11	16-26	22-36	30-50	40-60	
Physical Development – Moving and Handling:					
0-11	16-26	22-36	30-50	40-60	
Physical Development – Health and Self-care:					
0-11	16-26	22-36	30-50	40-60	

Summary of useful strategies and other things to know: (eg. staff training, equipment needed)

Agencies and services involved	List of documents attached
SENCO signature:	Parent/carer signature:

Chapter 10: Resources and training

Parent view

Child's name:	Date:
Parent's Name:	

Has your child made progress towards achieving their EHCP outcomes?

Are you happy with the support your child has received to achieve their EHCP outcomes?

What has gone well this year? Why do you think they have gone well?

What changes to existing outcomes/new outcomes would you like considered?

Did your family receive help from social care? If so, what support did you receive and was it successful?

Did your family receive help from health? If so, what support did you receive and was it successful?

Has your family been supported by a Special Educational Needs support service such as SENDIASS or any other organisations? If so, what support did you receive?

What are your aspirations for your child next year?

What are your hopes for your child after they finish their education?

Do you feel that your views and aspirations are accurately reflected in your child's EHCP?

Do you know about the Local Offer? YES/NO   *local offer website to be inserted here:*

Parent's signature:	Date:

Sample Provision Map

Child's name: Fred Smith

Setting: Messy Hands Nursery

Date of birth: 14.2.15

Identified need	Intervention	Description	Delivery style	Cost per session	Calculations explained	Effectiveness of provision
Fred finds it difficult to make himself understood by others.	Speech and language therapist	The nursery has one speech and language therapist who is working with Fred on the muscles involved with producing speech.	1:1 sessions	Anytown County Council NHS Trust	Service provided by NHS.	There has been some improvement as Fred does not have to repeat himself so often.
Fred finds it difficult to follow instructions and his language is delayed.	Early Years Talkboost and small group speaking and listening sessions.	Trained practitioner delivers speaking and listening interventions – Early Years Talkboost and speaking and listening activities with a small group of children.	1:1 and small group sessions (1:4)	30 minute session = £5.00 Resources = £3.00 per session Total = £8.00	Hourly practitioner rate: £10.00 £3.00 for resources covers photocopying and purchasing specialist resources.	Fred can follow an instruction with two information carrying words but doesn't always do so. He finds it difficult to answer questions and his sentences are not growing in length.

EHCP Review Timescales

Timescale	Action	Law
Two weeks before the start of each term	The local authority identifies which children need an EHCP review and contact schools and settings.	Children and Families Act 2014, Section 44 (1)
Every 12 months	The local authority has a statutory duty to complete a review for every child or young person with an EHC Plan. In some circumstances reviews may be carried out earlier.	'Local authorities have a duty to review EHC plans as a minimum every twelve months, and early years providers must co-operate in these reviews.' Early Years: guide to SEND Code of Practice 0-25, p.23
Every 11 months, ideally	The school or setting arrange the child's yearly EHCP review. Until the child attends school, it is the local authority's responsibility to make sure it happens, but the setting normally makes the arrangements as they are known to the family. Arrangements need to be made in good time to ensure relevant professionals can attend, professional reports and evidence of the child's progress towards EHCP targets are collated in time, and the parent's and child's views are documented.	Special Educational Needs and Disability Regulations 2014, Section 20 (3) – notice for attendance of EHCP reviews must be at least 2 weeks. Special Educational Needs and Disability Regulations 2014, Section 20 (1) – who must be invited to attend the meeting.
Up to 2 weeks before the meeting	The school or setting circulates copies of all relevant reports and paperwork to those invited to the meeting.	Special Educational Needs and Disability Regulations 2014, Section 20 (4)
During the EHCP review meeting	The review meeting must focus on: ● The child's progress towards achieving EHCP outcomes. ● Whether the outcomes and supporting targets are still appropriate. ● Reviewing the provision made for the child to ensure it continues to facilitate the child's progress towards educational, health and social targets. ● Whether or not the EHCP needs to continue in the light of the child's progress. ● Whether any outcomes or provision should be changed. ● Setting new outcomes for the coming year. ● Reviewing any personal budget arrangements which includes the statutory requirement to review direct payments.	Special Educational Needs and Disability Regulations 2014, Section 19
Within 2 weeks of the review meeting	After the EHC Plan review meeting, the school or maintained nursery school must prepare and send an annual review report of the meeting along with any other reports to everyone who was invited to the meeting (whether or not they attended). In the case of preschool settings other than maintained nursery schools, it is the local authority's responsibility to prepare the report. The annual review report must be sent to the local authority.	Special Educational Needs and Disability Regulations 2014, Section 20 (8) Early years: guide to SEND Code 0-25, p.23
Within 4 weeks of the review meeting	The local authority must decide whether it will make changes to the EHCP in light of the annual review report and they must notify the child's parents and the school/setting attended. The local authority must: ● Send the child's parents a copy of the existing EHCP with any amendments, together with supporting evidence. ● Inform the child's parents that they can request a meeting with an officer of the local authority. ● Inform the child's parents that they have 15 calendar days to request changes and make representations.	Special Educational Needs and Disability Regulations 2014, Section 20 (10). Special Educational Needs and Disability Regulations 2014, Section 22 (1) (c)
Within 8 weeks of sending the notice	The local authority issues a final version of the EHCP. They inform the child's parents of their right to appeal and their time limits for doing so and of the requirement for them to consider mediation. The local authority must make parents aware of the information, advice and support services available to them in the area.	Special Educational Needs and Disability Regulations 2014, Section 22 (3).

EHCNA and EHCP Timescales

Week	Action	Law
Week 0	Request is made to local authority for an EHCNA. The local authority becomes responsible for the child.	Section 36 Children and Families Act 2014 Section 24 Children and Families Act 2014
Week 6	EHCNA starts. The local authority must gather advice and information about the child's needs, the provision needed to support those needs and the outcomes that are expected as a result of provision.	Advice required and from whom: SEND Regs 2014: Regulation 6(1) 6-week time limit for advice to be sent to the local authority after request. SEND Regulations 2014 Reg.8(1) SEND Regs 2014: Regulation 6(4).
Week 14	A draft EHCP must have been produced (if the local authority agrees that it is needed) and sent to the parents. The parent has 15 calendar days to request changes or amendments.	Parent's right to respond to the draft of the EHCP plan and request the school/setting: CAFA 2014 s38(2) Time allowed, info on schools and right to meeting: SEND Regulations 2014 Regulation 13(1)
Week 16	If the local authority decides not to grant an EHCP they must notify the parent by this date along with their right to appeal.	Time limit for notice of refusal of a plan within 16 weeks: SEND Regulations 2014 Regulation 10(1)
Week 16	If the child does not already attend a school or setting, the local authority must contact the school/setting the parents want the child to attend by this time. The school/setting must respond within 15 calendar days.	CAFA 2014 s39(2) School response time limit: SEND Code paragraph 9.83
Week 20	Final EHCP issued by the local authority. The deadline from the request of assessment/ the local authority becoming responsible, to the local authority finalising the EHCP is 20 weeks, subject to limited exceptions.	SEND Regulations 2014: Regulation 13(2)

Record of Services

Service name	Service they provide	Contact name	Contact details	Notes

 Special Educational Needs and Disability (SEND) in practice

Practical resources

The following websites provide a wealth of resources that you can use to support children with a range of learning needs.

Communication Packs

Total Communication Resource Pack: https://www.eastsussex.gov.uk/media/3428/totalcommunicationresourcepackopt.pdf

The Communication Trust:
http://www.thecommunicationtrust.org.uk/early-years

Personal communication passports

A personal communication passport is a practical guide explaining how to communicate with a non-verbal child. It contains all the personal information about their specific needs, likes and dislikes. The passport is owned by the child themselves.

Scope's guide to creating a communication passport, which includes a template: https://www.cen.scot.nhs.uk/wp-content/uploads/2017/02/Scope_communication_passport.pdf

Sign language

Makaton: https://www.makaton.org/
Makaton is a type of sign language (as used by Mr Tumble on CBeebies). Makaton provides a visual representation of language which makes communication easier for young children.

British Sign Language (BSL): https://www.british-sign.co.uk/
A sign language system used mostly by people who are deaf or have a hearing impairment.

Social stories

Social stories help children to gain a greater social understanding. You can create and tailor social stories to suit a particular child.

How to Write a Social Story, Vanderbilt Kennedy Center
https://vkc.mc.vanderbilt.edu/assets/files/tipsheets/socialstoriestips.pdf

Social stories, ABA Educational Resources
https://www.abaresources.com/social-stories/

Springwell School: https://www.springwellschool.net/coronavirus-social-stories/
Age-appropriate stories and symbols specifically related to the coronavirus.

Visual aids

National Autistic Society:https://www.autism.org.uk/about/strategies/visual-supports.aspx
Visual supports to print out including symbols, instruction strips for using the bathroom, visual timetables and more.

Picture Communication System (PECS): https://pecs-unitedkingdom.com
This is a system of visual communication widely used in the UK. PECS also provides training for professionals in using the system.

Visuals2Go: https://www.visuals2go.com/
Create visuals for children with a range of communication needs.

Home learning

Hungry Little Minds: https://hungrylittleminds.campaign.gov.uk/
'Simple, fun activities for kids from newborn to five.'

Institute of Education: https://www.ucl.ac.uk/ioe/departments-and-centres/centres/centre-inclusive-education/homeschooling-children-send
Advice and links to practical resources parents can use with their children at home.

Speech and Language Kids: https://www.speechandlanguagekids.com/free-speech-language-resources/
Free speech and language resources as well as ways to help children with sensory or behavioural challenges.

Speechlink Parent Portal: https://speechandlanguage.info/parents
Blogs and videos to help parents support their child's talking as well as games and activities.

Chapter 10: Resources and training

The Autism Page: https://www.theautismpage.com/ Everything from printable visuals and children's activities to advice on therapies and completing SEND paperwork.

For children who are away from the setting for a long time having the chance to keep in regular touch with their key worker can make a big difference. It helps maintain a sense of normality and routine as well as supporting their eventual transition back to the setting. It also gives the keyworker the chance to see how the child is getting on and what adaptations and resource provision could make a difference. Software such as SchoolCloud (https://www.parentseveningsystem.co.uk/features-video-meetings.asp) is available free at the time of writing.

Organisations providing support

Action for Kids: https://www.my-afk.org/ This is mainly a charity for older children but they also 'provide mobility equipment not available on the NHS to disabled children and young people up to age 25 across the UK'.

Brainwave: https://www.brainwave.org.uk Brainwave helps children with SEND 'to achieve greater independence by aiming to improve mobility, communication skills and learning potential through a range of educational and physical therapies'.

Carers Trust: https://carers.org/ 'We offer specialist services for carers of people of all ages and conditions and a range of individually tailored support and group activities.'

Carers UK: https://www.carersuk.org/ 'Making life better for carers.'

Contact for families with disabled children: https://contact.org.uk/ 'We support families with the best possible guidance and information. We bring families together to support each other. And we help families to campaign, volunteer and fundraise to improve life for themselves and others.'

Council for Disabled Children: https://councilfordisabledchildren.org.uk/

The 'umbrella body for the disabled children's sector bringing together professionals, practitioners and policy-makers'.

Disability Rights UK: https://www.disabilityrightsuk.org/ A guide to benefits and services for disabled people of all ages and their carers.

Family Action: https://www.family-action.org.uk/ 'Family Action transforms lives by providing practical, emotional and financial support for those who are experiencing poverty, disadvantage and emotional isolation across the country'. The Duchess of Cambridge is their Patron.

Home-Start UK: https://www.home-start.org.uk/ 'Home-Start is a local community network of trained volunteers and expert support helping families with young children through their challenging times.'

IASS (Special Educational Needs and Disabilities Information, Advice and Support Service) is a free, confidential, impartial service for parents, carers and children. https://www.kids.org.uk/sendiass

IPSEA (Independent Parental Special Education Advice) offers free, independent advice on the SEND legal framework to parents, carers and professionals. https://www.ipsea.org.uk/

Mencap: https://www.mencap.org.uk/ Providing comprehensive, tailored advice about all aspects of special educational needs and disabilities. Their service includes a learning disabilities helpline.

https://nasen.org.uk/training-and-cpd/early-years/early-years-transition-webcasts.html

National Network of Parent Carer Forums (NNPCF): http://www.nnpcf.org.uk/ Lists around 152 local parent carer forums across England.

National Portage Association: https://www.portage.org.uk/support/region 'A (free) home-visiting educational service for preschool children with SEND and their families'.

Newlife: https://newlifecharity.co.uk/
Transforming lives by providing equipment for children with disabilities.

Scope: https://www.scope.org.uk/advice-and-support/
Scope provides 'practical information and emotional support when it's most needed'.

Skybadger: https://skybadger.co.uk/
Provides wide-ranging advice for parents and professionals, covering everything from writing EHCPs and organising finances to finding the right holiday.

Special Kids in the UK: http://specialkidsintheuk.org/
Aims to 'bring families (of children with SEND) together for friendship, to share information and to support one another'.

The Challenging Behaviour Foundation: https://www.challengingbehaviour.org.uk/
'Making a difference to the lives of people with severe learning disabilities.'

The Children's Sleep Charity: Leaflets: https://www.thechildrenssleepcharity.org.uk/leaflets.php
Working to help families enjoy the benefit of a good night's sleep.

The Percy Bilton Charity: http://www.percy-bilton-charity.org/
Providing grants for 'disadvantaged youth, people with disabilities, people with mental health problems and older people'.

Tourism for all: https://www.tourismforall.org.uk/
Specialising in accessible holidays for disabled people of all ages.

Winston's Wish: https://www.winstonswish.org/supporting-children-with-send/
Bereavement support for children with SEND

SEND training for practitioners

Local authorities often run general and more specific courses on supporting children with special educational needs and disabilities, as well as behaviour management courses. The easiest way to find what's on offer to you locally is probably to use a search engine.

For example, to find Cambridgeshire's courses we typed 'cambridgeshire courses for early years practitioners', and found the catalogue: https://www.cambslearntogether.co.uk/early-years-workforce-development-and-training-1

Here is a list of other course providers:

Cambridge Open College: https://cambridgeopencollege.ac/study/childcare-and-education/sen-teaching-assistant/
SEN Teaching Assistant (Level 3).

EduCare:https://www.educare.co.uk/courses/supporting-children-with-send
Online course – Supporting Children with SEND in the Early Years.

EYPS Services: https://www.eypservices.com/send-early-years-online-training-course/
SEND early years online training course.

IPSEA: https://www.ipsea.org.uk/
Independent provider of information, advice and support for parents, carers and practitioners. They also provide training for parents and professionals.

National Association for Special Needs (NASEN): https://nasen.org.uk/
'Supports all education practitioners by providing relevant Continuing Professional Development (CPD), resources, advice, information and much more to enable staff to meet the needs of all pupils including pupils with learning differences.'

National Day Nurseries Association (NDNA): https://www.ndna.org.uk/NDNA/Shop/previews/Early_years_SEND_online_training.aspx?utm_source=informz&utm_medium=sales_email&utm_campaign=sales_email_09_10_2018
They provide online courses for members.

Open Study College: https://www.openstudycollege.com/variant/sen
Special Educational Needs SEN (Level 3).

You can also use the Findcourses.co.uk website to find what you're looking for. Here are their links to SEND and behaviour management courses:

https://www.findcourses.co.uk/search/special-educational-needs-sen-training-courses

https://www.findcourses.co.uk/search/training-courses?q=behaviour%20management

National organisations for at least the majority of SEND conditions offer general and tailored training for practitioners in the early years and free, downloadable resources.

Legislation

Breaks for Carers of Disabled Children Regulations 2011
http://www.legislation.gov.uk/uksi/2011/707/contents/made

Children Act 1989
https://www.legislation.gov.uk/ukpga/1989/41/contents

Children and Families Act 2014 – Part 3
http://www.legislation.gov.uk/ukpga/2014/6/contents/enacted

Children Act 2004: http://www.legislation.gov.uk/ukpga/2004/31/contents
Children and Social Work Act 2017: http://www.legislation.gov.uk/ukpga/2017/16/contents/enacted
Education Act 1996 (Section 509A)
http://www.legislation.gov.uk/ukpga/1996/56/section/509A

Equality Act 2010
https://www.legislation.gov.uk/ukpga/2010/15/contents

Special Needs and Disability Regulations 2014
http://www.legislation.gov.uk/uksi/2014/1530/contents/made

The Children and Families Act 2014 Part 3: children and young people with educational needs and disabilities – A briefing from the Council of Disabled Children
https://councilfordisabledchildren.org.uk/sites/default/files/uploads/documents/import/ChildrenAndFamiliesActBrief.pdf

The Special Educational Needs (Personal Budgets) Regulations 2014
https://www.legislation.gov.uk/ukdsi/2014/9780111114056

The United Nations Convention on the Rights of People with Disabilities (CRPD)
https://www.un.org/development/desa/disabilities/convention-on-the-rights-of-persons-with-disabilities.html

UN Convention on the Rights of the Child (UNCRC)
https://www.unicef.org.uk/what-we-do/un-convention-child-rights/

Government guidance

Additional support for learning statutory guidance: 2017 (Scotland)
https://www.gov.scot/publications/supporting-childrens-learning-statutory-guidance-education-additional-support-learning-scotland/

Channel guidance (part of the Prevent Duty): https://assets.publishing.service.gov.uk/government/uploads/system/uploads/attachment_data/file/425189/Channel_Duty_Guidance_April_2015.pdf

Early education and childcare: statutory guidance for local authorities, 2018
https://assets.publishing.service.gov.uk/government/uploads/system/uploads/attachment_data/file/718179/Early_education_and_childcare-statutory_guidance.pdf

Early Years Foundation Stage Statutory Framework (EYFS)
https://www.gov.uk/government/publications/early-years-foundation-stage-framework--2

Early Years Foundation Stage Profile 2020 Handbook:
https://assets.publishing.service.gov.uk/government/uploads/system/uploads/attachment_data/file/856885/EYSP_handbook_2020.pdf

Early years entitlements: local authority funding of providers 2019-2020
https://assets.publishing.service.gov.uk/government/uploads/system/uploads/attachment_data/file/758271/EYNFF_Operational_Guide_-_2019-20_Final.pdf

Early years: guide to the 0-25 SEND code of practice
https://www.gov.uk/government/publications/send-guide-for-early-years-settings

Early Years Inspection Handbook for Ofsted registered provision, 2019
https://assets.publishing.service.gov.uk/government/uploads/system/uploads/attachment_data/file/828465/Early_years_inspection_handbook.pdf

Early years national funding formula: funding rates and guidance: https://www.gov.uk/government/publications/early-years-national-funding-formula-allocations-and-guidance

References

Early Years Pupil Premium (EYPP), Oxfordshire County Council
https://www.oxfordshire.gov.uk/business/
information-providers/childrens-services-providers/
support-early-years-providers/business-and-funding-
childcare-providers/early-education-fund/early-years-
pupil-premium

High needs funding 2018-2019: operational guide:
https://www.gov.uk/government/publications/high-
needs-funding-arrangements-2018-to-2019

Keeping children safe in education: statutory
guidance for schools and colleges, September 2019,
Department for Education: https://assets.publishing.
service.gov.uk/government/uploads/system/uploads/
attachment_data/file/835733/Keeping_children_safe_
in_education_2019.pdf

National Framework for Children and Young People's
Continuing Care: https://assets.publishing.service.gov.
uk/government/uploads/system/uploads/attachment_
data/file/499611/children_s_continuing_care_Fe_16.pdf

Ofsted Early Years Inspection Handbook 2019
https://www.gov.uk/government/publications/early-
years-inspection-handbook-eif

Ofsted: the education inspection framework, 2019
https://assets.publishing.service.gov.uk/government/
uploads/system/uploads/attachment_data/file/801429/
Education_inspection_framework.pdf

Prevent Duty, HM Government:https://assets.
publishing.service.gov.uk/government/uploads/system/
uploads/attachment_data/file/445977/3799_Revised_
Prevent_Duty_Guidance__England_Wales_V2-
Interactive.pdf

Safeguarding Disabled Children: Practice Guidance,
Department for Children, Schools and Families and
The Children's Society, 2009: https://assets.publishing.
service.gov.uk/government/uploads/system/uploads/
attachment_data/file/190544/00374-2009DOM-EN.pdf

SEND code of practice: 0-25 years
https://www.gov.uk/government/publications/send-
code-of-practice-0-to-25

SEND: guide for health professionals
https://www.gov.uk/government/publications/send-
guide-for-health-professionals

SEND: guide for parents and carers
https://www.gov.uk/government/publications/send-
guide-for-parents-and-carers

Short breaks for carers of disabled children
https://assets.publishing.service.gov.uk/government/
uploads/system/uploads/attachment_data/file/245580/
Short_Breaks_for_Carers_of_Disabled_Children.pdf

Short breaks for disabled children
https://www.gov.uk/government/publications/short-
breaks-for-disabled-children

Sources of income for early years providers
https://www.gov.uk/government/publications/early-
years-business-sustainability-guides-for-providers/extra-
sources-of-income-for-early-years-providers

Special Educational Needs Code of Practice for Wales
https://learning.gov.wales/docs/learningwales/
publications/131016-sen-code-of-practice-for-wales-
en.pdf

Working Together to Safeguard Children 2018,
Department for Education:
https://assets.publishing.service.gov.uk/government/
uploads/system/uploads/attachment_data/file/779401/
Working_Together_to_Safeguard-Children.pdf

Working Together: transitional guidance, July 2018, HM
Government:
https://assets.publishing.service.gov.uk/government/
uploads/system/uploads/attachment_data/file/722306/
Working_Together-transitional_guidance.pdf

Coronavirus guidance

Actions for early years and childcare providers during
the coronavirus (COVID-19) outbreak, Department for
Education:
https://www.gov.uk/government/publications/
coronavirus-covid-19-early-years-and-childcare-
closures/coronavirus-covid-19-early-years-and-
childcare-closures

Education, health and care needs assessments and plans: guidance on temporary legislative changes relating to coronavirus (COVID-19), updated 6th July 2020, Department for Education: https://www.gov.uk/government/publications/safe-working-in-education-childcare-and-childrens-social-care

Safe working in education, childcare and children's social care, Department for Education: https://www.gov.uk/government/publications/safe-working-in-education-childcare-and-childrens-social-care

Supporting vulnerable children and young people during the coronavirus (COVID-19) outbreak, Department for Education: https://www.gov.uk/government/publications/coronavirus-covid-19-guidance-on-vulnerable-children-and-young-people

Other sources

A guide to sensory stories: teachers' resource, BookTrust https://www.booktrust.org.uk/globalassets/resources/spark/teachers-resource.pdf

Annual Reviews, Contact https://contact.org.uk/advice-and-support/education-learning/ehc-plans-assessments/annual-reviews/

ASD and school trips, SEN Special Educational Needs https://senmagazine.co.uk/articles/articles/senarticles/asd-and-school-trips

Assess, plan, do, review: The graduated approach to SEN, SecEd http://www.sec-ed.co.uk/best-practice/assess-plan-do-review-the-graduated-approach-to-sen/

Bank of teaching strategies: Teacher Intervention and Differentiation Wave 1 https://www.dronfield.derbyshire.sch.uk/site_content/unsecure/sen/SEND-bank-of-teaching-strategies.pdf

Bristol's Local Offer, Portage Home Visiting Service https://www.bristol.gov.uk/web/bristol-local-offer/portage-home-visiting-service

British Association of Prosthetists & Orthotists https://www.bapo.com/

British Psychological Society (BPS) https://www.bps.org.uk/

Chartered Society of Physiotherapy https://www.csp.org.uk/

Child and adolescent mental health services (CAMHS) https://www.nhs.uk/using-the-nhs/nhs-services/mental-health-services/child-and-adolescent-mental-health-services-camhs/

Children with special educational needs and disabilities (SEND), Gov.uk https://www.gov.uk/children-with-special-educational-needs/extra-SEN-help

Choosing children's play equipment, DLS https://www.dlf.org.uk/factsheets/choosing-childrens-play-equipment

Community Children's Health Partnership (CCHP) https://cchp.nhs.uk/cchp/clinicians/community-paediatricians-referral

Create your own sensory story in 7 steps, Mencap https://www.mencap.org.uk/blog/create-your-own-sensory-story-7-steps

Definitions and signs of child abuse, NSPCC Learning: https://learning.nspcc.org.uk/research-resources/briefings/definitions-signs-child-abuse/

Developing high-quality inclusive practices, Family and Childcare Trust https://www.family-action.org.uk/content/uploads/2018/06/inclusive_practices_report.pdf

Disabled Children and Young People and those with Complex Health Needs, Department for Education and Skills, 2004: https://www.londoncp.co.uk/files/al_serv_framewk_ch_yp_and_Maternity_Services_-_Disabled_Children_and_Young_People_complex_health_needs.pdf

Education and Health and Care (EHC) Needs Assessments, Contact https://contact.org.uk/advice-and-support/education-learning/ehc-plans-assessments/education-health-and-care-(ehc)-needs-assessments/

References

Family Nurse Partnership
https://fnp.nhs.uk/about-us/the-programme/

Female Genital Mutilation, NHS: https://www.nhs.uk/
conditions/female-genital-mutilation-fgm/

Getting an Education and Health and Care (EHC) Plan,
Contact
https://contact.org.uk/advice-and-support/education-
learning/ehc-plans-assessments/getting-an-ehc-draft-
plan/

Getting social care services when your child has
additional needs, Contact a Family
https://contact.org.uk/media/1159919/getting_social_
care_services.pdf

Graduated Approach for children with SEND, Wigan
Council
https://www.wigan.gov.uk/Business/Professionals/Early-
Years-and-Childcare/Childcare-for-Children-with-Special-
Educational-Needs.aspx

Guide to childcare for children with special educational
needs and disabilities in England, Coram Family and
Childcare
https://www.familyandchildcaretrust.org/guide-childcare-
children-special-educational-needs-and-disabilities-
england

Health and Care Professions Council (HCPC)
https://www.hcpc-uk.org/

Inclusive Language: words to avoid and use when writing
about disability
https://www.gov.uk/government/publications/inclusive-
communication/inclusive-language-words-to-use-and-
avoid-when-writing-about-disability

Institute of Health Visiting (IHV), What is a health visitor?
https://ihv.org.uk/families/what-is-a-hv/

Local Government and Social Care Ombudsman
https://www.lgo.org.uk/make-a-complaint/fact-sheets/
education/special-educational-needs

My Space: Creating enabling environments for young
children, Oxfordshire County Council

https://www2.oxfordshire.gov.uk/cms/sites/default/
files/folders/documents/childreneducationandfamilies/
informationforchildcareproviders/Toolkit/My_Space_
Creating_enabling_environments_for_young_children.pdf

National Portage Association,
https://www.portage.org.uk/about/what-portage

Nature Play at Home by Nancy Striniste, Timber Press,
2019

NHS: Children and young people's services
https://www.nhs.uk/conditions/social-care-and-support-
guide/caring-for-children-and-young-people/children-
and-young-peoples-services/

Plants for a sensory garden, RHS Campaign for School
Gardening
https://schoolgardening.rhs.org.uk/resources/info-sheet/
plants-for-a-sensory-garden

Programmes that boost children's development rated,
Nursery World, Monday July 11th 2016
https://www.nurseryworld.co.uk/nursery-world/
news/1158168/programmes-that-boost-childrens-
development-rated

Refused an assessment for an EHCP? The Good
Schools Guide
https://www.goodschoolsguide.co.uk/special-
educational-needs/legal/refusal-to-assess-for-an-ehcp

Royal College of Occupational Therapists
https://www.rcot.co.uk/

Royal Collage of Paediatrics and Child Health
https://www.rcpch.ac.uk/

SEN and disability the early years: A toolkit, Council for
Disabled Children
https://councilfordisabledchildren.org.uk/sites/default/
files/uploads/documents/import/early-years-toolkit-
merged.pdf

Social care commentary: protecting disabled children,
Ofsted's National Director, Social Care, Eleanor
Schooling: https://www.gov.uk/government/speeches/
social-care-commentary-october-2017

Social Care in England: A Guide for Parents, Cerebra
https://cerebra.org.uk/wp-content/uploads/2019/11/
social-care-england-aug-19.pdf

Taking autistic pupils on a school trip, National Autistic
Society https://www.autism.org.uk/professionals/
teachers/theatre-and-museum.aspx

The Annual Review Process, IPSEA
https://www.ipsea.org.uk/the-annual-review-process

The Association of UK Dieticians (BDA)
https://www.bda.uk.com/

The British Association of Social Workers (BASW)
https://www.basw.co.uk/

The Royal College of Speech and Language Therapists
(RCSLT)
https://www.rcslt.org/-/media/Project/RCSLT/rcslt-early-
years-factsheet.pdf

The Significance of "The Doll Test", LDF
https://www.naacpldf.org/ldf-celebrates-60th-
anniversary-brown-v-board-education/significance-doll-
test/

Transitions for disabled children and children with SEN,
Council for Disabled Children
https://www.foundationyears.org.uk/files/2015/06/
Section-10-Transitions.pdf

Transport – children under five, IPSEA
https://www.ipsea.org.uk/children-under-5

What is an ECNO? Cambridgeshire County Council,
2014
https://learntogether-live.storage.googleapis.com/upload/
ENCo%20Handbook/ENCO_Sample_for_LTC.pdf

What is early intervention?, Early Intervention Foundation
https://www.eif.org.uk/why-it-matters/what-is-early-
intervention/

What should a good EHCP look like? The Good Schools
Guide
https://www.goodschoolsguide.co.uk/special-
educational-needs/legal/education-health-and-care-plans

What to do if you're worried a child is being abused:
advice for practitioners, HM Government, March 2015
https://assets.publishing.service.gov.uk/government/
uploads/system/uploads/attachment_data/file/419604/
What_to_do_if_you_re_worried_a_child_is_being_
abused.pdf

Working with Deaf and Physically Disabled Children
and Young People in Relation to Child Sexual
Abuse and Other Forms of Exploitation: A Toolkit for
Professionals, The Children's Society: https://www.
csepoliceandprevention.org.uk/sites/default/files/tcs_
cse_physicaldisabilities_toolkit.pdf

References

Notes

1   Brain wiring could be behind learning difficulties, say experts, The Guardian, https://www.theguardian.com/science/2020/feb/27/brain-wiring-could-be-behind-learning-difficulties-say-experts?CMP=share_btn_link&fbclid=IwAR2e_A0B9a9LbIIVEWESpgPnHIFoU6D4k_jYtRHU9el5Jv4AtqeOdRzQvdg

2   Diagnostic and Statistical Manual of Mental Disorders (DSM), American Psychiatric Association, https://www.psychiatry.org/psychiatrists/practice/dsm

3   Why many autistic girls are overlooked, Child Mind Institute, https://childmind.org/article/autistic-girls-overlooked-undiagnosed-autism/

4   5 headline changes to the New Ofsted Inspection Framework, Third Space Learning, https://thirdspacelearning.com/blog/new-ofsted-framework-2019-inspection-changes/#4

5   National Health Service Act 2006, http://www.legislation.gov.uk/ukpga/2006/41/contents

6   Reasonable adjustments for disabled children, Equality and Human Rights Commission https://www.equalityhumanrights.com/en/publication-download/reasonable-adjustments-disabled-pupils

7   'SEND no longer the poor relation during an Ofsted inspection', The Schools, Students and Teachers Network (SSAT): https://www.ssatuk.co.uk/blog/send-no-longer-the-poor-relation-during-an-ofsted-inspection/

8   The Breaks for Carers of Disabled Children Regulations 2011 http://www.legislation.gov.uk/uksi/2011/707/made

9   Why we're doing too much, too young in education, John Severs, 5th February 2020, TES, https://www.tes.com/news/why-were-doing-too-much-too-young-education

10 Schools and Early Years Finance Regulations 2018, Section 11: http://www.legislation.gov.uk/uksi/2018/10/regulation/11/made

11 Here's why children need to play with inclusive dolls, Motherhood: The real deal, https://motherhoodtherealdeal.com/parenthood/heres-why-children-need-to-play-with-inclusive-dolls/

12 Children – research and statistics, Mencap, https://www.mencap.org.uk/learning-disability-explained/research-and-statistics/children-research-and-statistics

13 British Sign Language (BSL), https://www.british-sign.co.uk/bsl-greetings-signs-british-sign-language/

14 Makaton, https://www.makaton.org/

15 Makaton, https://www.makaton.org/

16 Picture Exchange Communication System (PECS), https://pecs-unitedkingdom.com/pecs/

17 Joseph Rowntree Foundation, 'Special educational needs and their links to poverty':https://www.jrf.org.uk/report/special-educational-needs-and-their-links-poverty

Acknowledgements

We would like to thank Celia Phipps, Portage Home Visitor, and Pam Pantazi from Little Hands Nursery, for sharing their knowledge and answering all of our questions. A big thank you to all the early years practitioners who shared their views about how practitioners would like to be supported to help children with SEND, especially Irina Savulescu, Level 3 nursery practitioner and SEND teaching assistant, and Leisha Hopgood, SEND 1:1 preschool worker.

Special thanks to Kirstie Latte who allowed Claire to attend her son Michael's EHCP review meeting.

We would also like to thank the Child and Family Centre in Cambourne for the help and information they provided.

Particular thanks to Pinpoint Cambridgeshire local parent/carer forum, the Special Educational Needs and Disabilities Information, Advice and Support Services (SENDIASS) in Cambridgeshire, and Contact for the amazing workshops that enriched our knowledge.

Our thanks go to all the parents and carers around the UK who have shared their experiences and knowledge with us, increasing our determination to write this book, especially to those who attend the Cambridge babies and children with Down Syndrome support group and the Additional Needs Parents Support group in Papworth Everard, Cambridgeshire.

Thank you to all the charity organisations and associations related to each condition. Their websites and helplines were invaluable to us. We would also like to thank all the health and care professionals, specialists and clinicians who took the time to talk to us and guide us through special educational needs and disabilities processes.

A very warm and special thank you to Claudia's daughter Sophie, who is the inspiration for this book.